Babes in the Woods

Help Us Keep This Guide Up to Date

Every effort has been made by the author and editors to make this guide as accurate and useful as possible. However, many things can change after a guide is published—regulations change, techniques evolve, etc.

We would love to hear from you concerning your experiences with this guide and how you feel it could be improved and kept up to date. While we may not be able to respond to all comments and suggestions, we'll take them to heart, and we'll also make certain to share them with the author. Please send your comments and suggestions to the following address:

The Globe Pequot Press
Reader Response/Editorial Department
P.O. Box 480
Guilford, CT 06437

Or you may e-mail us at:

editorial@GlobePequot.com

Thanks for your input, and happy travels!

Babes in the Woods

The Woman's Guide to Eating Well, Sleeping Well,
and Having Fun in the Backcountry

Bobbi Hoadley

FALCON®

GUILFORD, CONNECTICUT
HELENA, MONTANA

AN IMPRINT OF THE GLOBE PEQUOT PRESS

Falcon and FalconGuide are registered trademarks of The Globe Pequot Press.

Cover photos: © Index Stock

Text design: Lisa Reneson

Library of Congress Cataloging-in-Publication Data
Hoadley, Bobbi.
    Babes in the woods : the woman's guide to eating well, sleeping well, and having fun in the backcountry / Bobbi Hoadley.—1st ed.
        p. cm.
    ISBN 0-7627-2530-3
    1. Outdoor recreation for women. 2. Camping. I. Title.

GV191.64.H63 2003
796'.082—dc21   2003044943

Manufactured in the United States of America
First Edition/First Printing

This book is dedicated to the Girl Guides of Canada/Guides du Canada, where girls just want to have fun.

Contents

Preface: Susanna Moodie Roughs It in the Bush   ix

Acknowledgments   xi

Introduction: What Is Women's Camping and Why Do It?   1
     Backcountry Camping Doesn't Have to Be Macho   2
       Camping Is Supposed to Be *Fun!*   2
     How to Camp like a Woman   3
       Being a Lightweight   3
       A Foodie on the Trail Is Worth Two in the Bush   5
     You Can Do It!   6

1. Ready, Set . . . You Go, Girl!   7
     Getting in Shape   7
       Shake, Rattle, and Roll—Body Mechanics   9
       How Fit Are You?—A Simple Test   9
     Get Some Attitude!   10
     Choose a Destination   11
       Start Small   11
       Going Farther Afield   12
     Be Safe   13
       First Aid   13
       Wildlife   14

2. Getting in Gear   15
     Get Organized   15
       Group Gear   16
       Checklists for Everything; or, Time Management 101   17
     Equipment Acumen   18
       Backpacks   18
       Sleeping Bags and Sleeping Pads   19
       Tents and Tarps   21
     Personal Items   23
       Fashion Sense   24

3. Weathering the Weather   27
     Weather Forecasting   27
       Everyone Knows It's Windy   28
       Watch the Clouds   28

Keeping Dry   28

    Port in a Storm   29

Keeping Toasty   30

Campfire or Not?   31

    The Downside   31

    Minimum-Impact Fires   32

4. Hygiene Hoodwinks   **35**

A Wash on the Wild Side   35

The Joys of a Cat Hole   36

    Digging the Hole   37

    Covering Your Tracks   37

Or Try This   37

5. Eating Well   **39**

Your Portable Kitchen   39

Trail Nutrition   41

About Weight—in Your Pack   41

Food Preparation   42

    Stove Sensibilities   42

Gourmet Presentations   43

Water Purification   44

Meal Cleanup   45

6. Safety and First Aid   **47**

Basic First Aid—What to Know Before You Go   48

    Ailments   48

    Medication   53

How to Think on Your Feet   54

    Planning Ahead   54

    Confidence and Safety   54

    Assessing Risks   54

    Handling Emergencies with Resolve   56

Wildlife Wisdom   56

    Bear Aware!   56

7. The Art of Happy Camping   **59**

Group Fun   60

    Fun and Games   60

    Drinking   62

    Snack!   62

    Enjoy the Downtime   63

It's an Art   64

Epilogue: Leaving Susanna Behind   **65**

Appendix 1: Pack-and-Go Trail Recipes   **67**

Dehydrating Your Food   69

     Oven-Drying   70

Handling Dehydrated Food   71

Basic Recipes for Dehydrating Ingredients at Home   72

Bannock and Breakfast   76

     Making Bannock   76

     Other Breakfast Items   78

Lunch   82

Supper   86

Desserts   102

Other Make-at-Home Treats   105

Hot Drink Recipes   106

Appendix 2: Games   **109**

Terms to Know   109

Baffle Bridge   109

Durock   110

Hearts   111

Dingbat Poker   112

Dingbat Poker—Archie Version   113

Hopscotch   113

Five Stones   114

Appendix 3: The Checklists   **115**

Preparedness Checkup   115

Sample Kit List for Camping   117

Group Equipment List   119

Safety Support Kit   120

Wilderness First-Aid Kit Group Supplies   121

Long-Term Remote First-Aid Survey Checklist   123

About the Author   **125**

Preface: Susanna Moodie Roughs it in the Bush

I felt rather timid when I found myself with only my female companion in the vast forest, I kept my fears to myself, lest I should be laughed at. This foolish dread of encountering wild beasts in the woods I never could wholly shake off, even after becoming a constant resident in their gloomy depths. . . . The cracking of an old bough, or the hooting of the owl was enough to fill me with alarm, and try my strength in a precipitate flight. I could not overcome the weakness of the flesh. If I had one of my infants with me [it] gave me for a time fictitious courage; but it was like love fighting with despair. It was in vain that my husband assured me that no person had ever been attacked by wild animals in the woods; whilst I knew that wild animals existed in those woods, I could not believe him, and my fears rather increased than diminished.

— Susanna Moodie, *Roughing It in the Bush*

The doyenne of women in the backwoods, Susanna Moodie was as reluctant a backcountry camper as any I have encountered. She was unashamedly tied to her city life, social activities, and all the comforts of home. Mrs. Moodie states in the introduction to *Roughing It in the Bush* that "Few educated persons, accustomed to the refinements and luxuries of European society, will ever willingly relinquish those advantages and place themselves beyond the protective influence of the wise and revered institutions. . . ." In recounting her eight years of life in the Canadian backwoods, from 1832 to 1840, Susanna had none of the rosy optimism of the American pioneer Laura Ingalls Wilder, nor the heroism of Canadian Laura Secord in the

War of 1812. Susanna was often an unhappy camper, complaining bitterly of her life in the wilderness as her husband left her on her own while he went off soldiering.

Even though *Roughing It in the Bush* was written more than twenty years after Susanna Moodie's experiences in the backcountry, she remained ambivalent about them. Upon her return to "civilization," she lamented the loss of her "dear forest home which I had loved in spite of all the hardships which we had endured since we pitched our tent in the backwoods. It was . . . the school of high resolve and energetic action which we had learned to meet calmly, and successfully to battle with the ills of life."

During her sojourn in the bush, Susanna was regularly more offended by the bad manners of her neighbors and visitors than she was by her husband's abandonment. She maintained—in fact defended—her feminine sensibilities during her predicament and yet survived admirably. Through her tears, fears, and female fluttering, she single-handedly raised five children, fought two fires and a tornado, and survived numerous other life-threatening experiences, all while immensely enjoying the scenery.

Susanna Moodie's is still the voice of women in the backcountry. Unlike Susanna, we know that we can go home in a short time, and our labor is a lot more fun than subsistence farming. Susanna went hungry at times, and she really was "roughing it"; we don't have to accept her level of hardship. We can even eat well. In writing about her travails, Susanna understood that the effort, no matter how modest, *is* the accomplishment. It is clear that she was proud of herself and learned a great deal she'd never known was there to learn. Every woman I've ever camped with has felt the same way after a backcountry trip. We may not be as bold or heroic as we think we need to be. We may sweat the hardships and suffer the unknown. But like Susanna, we may also discover our inner strength and bring deeper meaning to our lives.

So if you wonder whether you can do it, and you're a little anxious and afraid, remember Susanna and read on. Tackle the adventure from a woman's perspective. After you've acknowledged your feelings, however, do what Susanna did and *get on with it.*

Acknowledgments

I want to acknowledge all the women and girls who have shared my experiences—especially the fun, the friendships, and the food. I wish I could name you all, but there are too many. Our happy memories resonate in the pages of this book. Thank you.

My friend Kathy Vanderlinden talked me into writing this book and then mentored me through the proposal and first edit. Her support and encouragement were invaluable.

Thanks to my editor, Erin Turner, who recognized my passion for this subject and cheered me on, making the writing process fun.

Finally, thank you to Peter, who always has kept the home fires burning.

Introduction: What is Women's Camping and Why Do It?

It's a sad, sad story: A woman comes back from a camping trip covered in bug bites and blisters, tired to the bone from having slept on a rock, hungry after eating gooey freeze-dried macaroni and cheese, and convinced that she hates hiking, camping, and possibly even the man who dragged her out into the woods.

The good news is—it doesn't have to be that way.

Camping has historically been a male-dominated activity, presumably because it's related to hunting and fishing, which are typically guy sports. It is time to recognize that camping has a "Mars–Venus" component. Since women have traditionally learned backcountry camping from men, not all of us have discovered a feminine perspective—but our day has come. Now that more and more people are heading into the wilderness, we women can reinvent our own role in the woods, as well.

In the twenty-first century, camping is no longer an activity for a few adventuresome souls; it's rather a way for many to escape the urban sprawl and stress. Advances in equipment, clothing, and communications technology have made camping an increasingly safe and popular activity. Campers can readily move into ever-more-remote areas to enjoy the beauty and peace of a pristine environment.

Naturally, women are exploring this new era, too. We are challenging both male rules and female fears and demonstrating the special joys of camping, female style, with high-tech comforts and a new set of ethics. We enjoy backcountry camping in very different ways from our male companions, using skills and practices that suit women and taking our own kind of pleasure from the wilds.

Backcountry camping is a wonderful, exciting activity, and there are novel ways of looking at it and doing it. We can reject the role of a naive traveler in a fearful environment, a "babe in the woods." If we assert our needs and deter-mine our own measure of enjoyment, then we have opened the door to the outdoors for good and all.

Backcountry Camping Doesn't Have to Be Macho

We are currently seeing an extraordinary overuse of superlatives to describe backcountry camping. Interaction with our environment is often characterized by marketing terms like *extreme, on the edge,* and *pumped*.

Not only do we talk big, we are encouraged to act big. Society attributes heroism to people for taking unreasonable risks in the name of outdoor enter-tainment. *Gladiators, Survivor, No Boundaries,* and even *Crocodile Hunter* are popular reality TV shows that exploit our fascination with risk. Yet such a pres-entation of heroism is misleading; even men are having difficulty keeping up with the image.

Perhaps men have unconsciously exaggerated the dangers of the wilder-ness to enhance their enjoyment in being there and increase its macho aroma. Men seem to be far more attracted to the adrenaline rush, which increases with perceived danger. Many women, on the other hand, will overdose on adrenaline rather quickly and want to go home. For us, the survival need says *Avoid all danger; protect yourself and your young*—and we listen.

Camping Is Supposed to Be *Fun!*

If you've never camped, you may find it almost impossible to imagine how this could be fun. It is equally difficult to explain what makes it so much fun. Much like losing your virginity, a leap of faith is required . . . and once you've done it right, you're sure to do it again. Indeed, many women who camp as adults were introduced to the experience as children, when everything we did and learned was a leap of faith.

Camping, particularly a moving camp or backcountry camp, provides oppor-tunities that are hard to reproduce in any other setting. It can be a deeply rewarding exercise in understanding and using effective life skills. When we live communally for extended periods of time without many of the lifestyle conveniences and distractions to which we are accustomed, we draw on our inner resources and gain valuable perspective on ourselves. Far from being stressful, a challenging camping experience actually seems to draw out the best in us.

It is with a heightened sensibility that we enjoy the experience, the beauty, and the fun. Women have at various times described "never feeling so alive," "never laughing so hard," and having "more fun than any party and without the booze!" Geniality and friendship flow from the shared experiences and accomplishments. Deep bonds develop quickly; it's hard to go home and leave behind the friends and the shared adventures. Camping friends become best friends, and memories are recalled for life. I have rarely known a woman to go camping because she wanted to toughen up or because she was just itching to "rough it"—testosterone may be a required ingredient in that kind of reasoning. We instead focus on comfort and ease, many of us insisting on it. This book thus offers ideas for experiencing the outdoors in a more comfortable, fun way. And at the risk of sounding like your mother: "If you sleep well and eat well, then you'll enjoy the experience more."

How to Camp like a Woman

Put an end to death marches under sixty-pound loads, throw out everything you've heard about the rigors and hardships of backcountry camping, and get ready to head into the backcountry with style, comfort, and plenty of fun.

In the 1960s, when feminism was gaining a toehold on the cultural scene in North America, women embraced the role of "earth mother." It fit with our view of ourselves as powerful and free—yet still fulfilling the caring and nurturing role we'd always played in society. It didn't take us long, however, to realize that this was just the same old servitude in a new dress.

Our struggles to find the right role since then have taken us into all kinds of places where we just didn't feel like we belonged because the rules there were made by men and for men. Our choices have been to adopt traditionally male attitudes and behaviors, which have left us feeling unfulfilled, or to go with our feelings and be misunderstood or sometimes disregarded.

Taking a trip "back to the earth" with a feminine perspective offers the opportunity to taste those "earth mother" roles that were so appealing way back when—only now the power and the freedom to be whom we choose to be is based on our preferences and generosity of spirit. Women traveling together will find that their personal goals are more readily achieved when they're tied to the group's goals.

Once you've mastered the art of camping like a woman, you may be able to teach the men in your life a thing or two. When the guys have tried it your way, they'll be looking for another chance to join you—at least some of the time.

Being a Lightweight

As we push on through our busy lives, it seems like we have fewer of those "take your breath away" experiences. An encounter with wilderness is never anticlimactic. But it will become rare if we don't unselfishly work to preserve or re-create the natural integrity of the backcountry. Women can become a

Treading Lightly

Planning a good, lightweight, minimum-impact camp must begin with the following essentials.

Do Your Research

Everyone deserves the opportunity to discover an untouched wilderness. Be prepared to do the kind of research required so that you leave no impact on your chosen site. Backcountry camping obliges us to examine our ecosystem and use practices appropriate to its geology, plant life, and wildlife, minimizing the long-term effects of our passing. When traveling in a fragile environment, planning ahead will help you travel as lightly as possible.

Coordinate Your Gear

The more coordinated and cooperative your group's efforts are, the better your camping practices will be. Women sometimes have a tendency to bring along numerous "just-in-case" items. If you list and pack the group's gear together and agree to share everything, you won't end up with a lot of unnecessary duplication and weight.

Act like a Guest

When you're in the backcountry, behave as though you are visiting a beautiful home (you are). Never pick, break, or take anything from the natural environment. Stay on the trails and use existing sites to camp on. Avoid shortcuts through vegetation, and don't pick the flowers or cut the foliage and trees. Leave what you find; you're not in a souvenir shop. Do not build or dig. Light fires only when necessary for emergency warmth or protection, and then know how to build them so that they can be cleared away with no traces left. Avoid making too much loud noise.

Haul Out Your Waste

The rule of thumb is, "If you pack it in, pack it out." When you leave a site, there should be no traces that you were there. Waste includes garbage, human waste, food waste, and wastewater. Keep track of everything that you use so that you don't abuse, overuse, or waste anything. Leave every site better than you found it.

For more information, the "Leave No Trace" Outdoor Skills and Ethics program sponsored by the National Outdoor Leadership School in the United States provides the most extensive and up-to-date information available. They have materials and resources that address specific ecosystems and teach a wide variety of no-trace skills. Visit their Web site at www.lnt.org or call (800) 332-4100.

positive and proactive force for the preservation and wise use of what's left of our wilderness, and strong advocates for backcountry ethics. We already adopt lightweight minimum-impact practices as a matter of course once we understand the reasoning and mechanics behind them.

A wealth of ads these days depict people in the backcountry with a car,

and the incongruence of this is never questioned. It seems as though everyone in North America wants to own a sport utility vehicle or a four-by-four. The
marketing around these vehicles is all about their "off-road capabilities." So
now your Sunday drive can involve damaging wildlife habitat and flora and
fauna that could take more than ten years to regenerate. All this smells of
more machismo to me.

The challenge in this century is to camp in ways that prevent or limit overuse of the natural environment. Even if we camp at established campsites or
buildings, minimum-impact camping practices are still important. Only if we
leave the natural environment intact can we continue to enjoy the richness
and diversity of life in the outdoors.

Environmental science has proven that our earth can thrive if we are an
undemanding audience. And while many men share these values and advo-
cate for the same outdoor ethics, the feminine perspective uniquely lends
itself to environmentalism and economy of use. We are less averse to being
"lightweights"; we already understand that sometimes it's the stronger role.

Lightweight camping is indeed a necessity for women, not only for environmental reasons but also for practical ones. A self-contained, moving backcountry camp requires that you be able to transport everything that you bring.
Very few women can manage to carry as much as a man can. This is a case
where less is definitely more—as long as you choose the "less" carefully. And
when your camping companions are all female, no one will make you feel like
a wimp for doing so. When you can be smug about ensuring your comfort and
ease minimally, you may give your male camping companions a more sane
perspective about excess.

Lightweight is a more cautious way to go because it is less interfering and
antagonistic to a wilderness environment. Yet we can adopt minimum-impact
camping practices for the backcountry without sacrificing comfort and style.
When we incorporate environmental ethics and conservationist standards into
the practice of backcountry travel, we can take nurturing to new levels.
Embracing environmental stewardship can be added to the list of unique
opportunities available to us through camping like a woman.

A Foodie on the Trail Is Worth Two in the Bush

For whatever reason, male-driven camp cookery suffered for years from the
three "Fs": fast, filling, and flavorless. With more women on the camping scene,
camping food has steadily improved, perhaps because more women have
become involved in the activity. The truth is, good food is crucial to the enjoyment of any outdoor activity, even if some of our men are willing to make do
with any food as long as they get enough. Without flavorful and interesting

food, almost everyone will become peckish and lose their good humor.

Buying packaged food is one option, but it is costly and not always appetizing. Preparing your own gourmet dehydrated meals is not difficult and will keep everyone on an even keel. Meals can be prepared so they cook quickly and without too much mess or fuss, and gourmet camp cookery is your opportunity to shine. If there is anyone who doesn't understand why you want to camp like a woman, one or two lightweight gourmet meals will "strut your stuff."

You Can Do It!

There are many things we do every day that are more dangerous than going on a wilderness camping expedition, including riding in the car to get there. In everything we do, we feel safer when we know the risks and how to safely manage them, and then become familiar with the task. It would be very dangerous to work in your kitchen if you knew nothing about stove fires, burns, electrical safety, scalding water, slippery floors, and sharp knives. It's equally dangerous to be in the backcountry if you don't know how to deal with wild animals, weather, hypothermia, and trail conditions. It's critical that we go into the backcountry with a thorough knowledge and understanding of the task at hand. If we have that, then we can leave our fears behind. The key to not getting psyched out is to get ready!

Finding the right combination of comfort, style, ethics, and good food guarantees fun. The all-woman camping experience may be a way to break into this new way of thinking—but once you've mastered it, do us all a favor and share it with the men in your life. Read on to see how to make it happen.

1 Ready, Set... You Go, Girl!

Just in case it wasn't absolutely clear in the introduction to this book, backcountry camping is supposed to be fun! But it won't be if you don't spend a little time in preparation before heading out into the woods. This chapter is about how to get yourself prepared—mentally and physically—for the rigors of the woods. It's also about how to make those rigors less rigorous and ... more fun. That's the whole idea. Once you've decided to go backcountry camping, expect to spend at least as much time in preparation as you did for your first date. Admit it: The final hour or two you spent primping for that date was really only a fraction of the time and energy you'd invested in getting to that point—rehearsing conversational topics, practicing facial expressions in the mirror, and doing a little bit of puckering up with your pillow, not to mention trying on everything you owned ... and a few things you didn't.

For your first backcountry camping trip, you'll be borrowing stuff, you'll be practicing stuff, and you may still have butterflies when you're ready to hit the trail. What follows is some of the basic information you'll need to successfully manage your camping adventures, plus some suggestions on avoiding a few major pitfalls. Use this chapter to keep yourself happy, healthy, and safe in the backcountry.

Eventually, you'll find better ways of doing things because they will be your *own* ways. My objective is to ensure that you don't screw up so badly, you never go again. Like the second or fifth date with the right person, camping won't lose its allure ... but the buildup to it *will* get streamlined.

Getting in Shape

In my experience as a fitness instructor, I have noticed that women consistently underestimate their physical abilities, possibly because of the male hyperbole that's often been attached to fitness and outdoor recreation. Regrettably, accepted activities for girls rarely include building upper-body strength, especially in their growth years and adolescence. But on the upside, given the steadily expanding opportunities for women to participate in competitive sports, many of us are learning to push our limits—and we're finding that they're much higher than we think. On a challenging camping trip, most women learn they are capable of much more than they thought.

Before heading out into the woods, though, it's wise to understand your own body mechanics and level of fitness. Remember: Fitness is the partner to skill if you want to get anywhere successfully.

Speaking of skill, if you're going to travel by any means other than hiking— perhaps via canoe, kayak, sail, bike, ski, or horseback—be sure you're proficient enough. It's a good idea to take lessons and practice your skills before you go. You may have paddled around the pond when you were a kid, ridden a horse a couple of times, or ridden a bike regularly, but that's much different from doing any of those things as a means of long-distance transportation. It takes very little time for insufficient skills to result in pain and injury. I once talked my friend Diana into joining a kayak trip on the Sechelt Inlet, a sheltered coastal fjord north of Vancouver, British Columbia. She was a seasoned camper and a good canoeist but had never done much ocean kayaking. After I'd reassured her that sixty-three was not too old to learn, she agreed to join our group of ten women and teenage girls for three days.

The first thing that was required of all the novice kayakers on our first afternoon was a wet exit. It's extremely difficult for many women to roll a fully loaded sea kayak. This exercise reassures the paddler that she can indeed get out of the kayak at will—and, subsequently, back in. Everyone was expected to roll the kayak over and hang upside down for at least thirty seconds while pounding on the hull of the boat to draw attention and then pulling the "panic loop" of the spray skirt to slide out of the kayak. Once everyone had exited, we could head up the inlet to the more remote sites.

Diana went last. She was clearly anxious and upset. I remembered my first wet exit only the year before, hanging upside down with the eelgrass and jelly-fish in my face, wondering what had possessed me to do such a thing. I tried to reassure my friend by telling her how easy it was to slide out of the kayak, but clearly she believed this to be just one more thing she was letting me talk her into doing . . . and at that moment, against her will. Yet I couldn't tip the kayak for her. She had to do it herself and she did, popping out and coming to the surface with a huge smile on her face. It was hard work climbing back in, but she was determined and managed it successfully.

We headed up the inlet in the afternoon sun with seals popping up around our little fleet as they chased and raced along with us. After a delicious supper of Spanish rice, Diana confided in me that she had not slept for a week worrying about that exercise. Not only that, but her entire family had been worried about her coming on the trip. We were both pretty glad that it hadn't stopped her.

Going out into the backcountry for an extended trip without adequate skills is comparable to wearing a new pair of shoes around the shoe store—and then walking around Europe in them. If you're counting on a new skill to get you where you want to go, practice a little first.

Shake, Rattle, and Roll—Body Mechanics

It's essential that women understand and accept their body mechanics. Don't let a man teach you how to lift, haul, or carry, because it's usually not possible for women to use the same muscles in the same ways as men. Even with strong arms, many of us don't have the build or muscle structure to exert force above the waist as well as a man can. Most women find that once their arms reach chest height, they lose strength. The higher a woman's arms go, the less force they're able to exert.

To compensate, take advantage of your center of gravity, which is lower than a man's. On the trail, you can try to maneuver weights to a lower height—for instance, by carrying a boat (portaging) at hip or waist height with a straight back, rather than over your head. And plan on using two women for a one-man task. When hiking, paddling, or carrying, make sure that your pelvis is forward to give you better balance and more strength and to protect your back. Do not lead with your chin and chest. Instead, throw your shoulders back, tuck in your butt, and flex your knees—that will push your pelvis forward.

How Fit Are You?—A Simple Test

Here's a quick test of strength, endurance, agility, balance, and aerobic capacity. When you get to the end, you'll have a better idea about your present abilities and the areas that might need work.

Perform these tests one after the other. You should be able to do each one easily, with good balance, good breath control, and a recovery time of less than a minute.

Strength

1. Keeping your back straight (use your leg muscles), lift thirty-five pounds from the ground to waist height three times.
2. Walk up and down a flight of stairs (at least twelve steps) carrying thirty-five pounds of weight three times.

How High Is Up?

At a 10 percent grade, it will take you twice as long to reach your destination as it would at your usual pace. Anything more than 20 percent could take four or five times longer.

To figure out from a topographic map the amount of climb in your hike:

• Count the contour lines to determine how many feet in vertical distance you'll be climbing. Each line equals 100 feet in elevation.

• Use a string to measure the trail and compare it with the map's scale to determine the length in horizontal distance you'll be traveling. Multiply miles (or fractions of) by 5,280 feet to get the distance in feet.

• Divide the elevation in feet by the length of the trail in feet (that is, divide step 1 by step 2) to get the percentage of grade you'll be climbing.

Agility

3. Run up and down a flight of stairs sideways (your back leg crossing every other step) five times on each side.

4. Get into a straight-backed chair (the back should be approximately 20 inches high) by climbing over the back of it five times without stepping on any rungs.

Endurance

5. Sit-ups (lie on your back, knees bent, hands at your temples, and lift your shoulders completely off the floor); do fifteen.

6. Push-ups (knees down): do fifteen.

Balance

7. Imagine a clock on the floor, with you in the center of it. Point your big toe at twelve, three, six, and nine o'clock going clockwise and then counterclockwise without losing your footing. Do both feet. Move as quickly as possible.

8. Standing on one foot, raise your knee to your chest, then take your heel to your bum, moving your leg as high as it will go front and back without losing your footing. Do both legs.

If these tasks are difficult for you, then you're probably not ready for a long overnight backpack or canoe trip. Start working on your fitness level first, and then plan a few short outings to get used to the activity you've chosen before heading out for three days with a pack on your back. Experts recommend an hour of exercise three times a week to ensure cardiac fitness—some even recommend an hour seven days a week to maintain tip-top form. Find your balance and get moving! An easier backpacking trip or canoe excursion will be your reward.

Get Some Attitude!

Once you have addressed fitness and skill, check out your attitude. It is attitude that defines the experience and the fun that you will have. Remember that the first half hour of strenuous exercise is the most difficult. After that, your body will find a rhythm, and if you know how to distract yourself from the physical labor, you'll accomplish your goals. If you're camping with women, distraction is a bit easier, because we are so often eager to talk. I like to sing and can often get my companions to join me.

Interact with your surroundings as well as your companions. Look around and outside yourself to smell the flowers and enjoy the view. Be mentally prepared to enjoy, entertain, and support your fellow campers and you'll find that you will have a better time. Adopt flexibility and humor as a reaction to the stressful times, and you'll be dauntless.

There's No Place like Home

TIP

If you're just starting out, close to home is best for several reasons. It's easier to get information about where you're going, for one thing. Also, you're more likely to be familiar with seasonal changes, possible weather concerns, wildlife, and other local hazards so you can do an effective job of risk management.

Choose a Destination

Your primary considerations as you select your destination or route will be your level of ability, drop-off and pickup arrangements (if you don't double back), the availability of rental equipment (if needed), and the availability of emergency assistance. Give yourself plenty of time to become familiar with where you're hoping to go, and if something doesn't make sense or concerns you, ask about it.

Start Small

I wish I had a hug for every time I've heard a story about people out in the wilderness who were in way over their heads. Usually the story goes from bad to worse and ends with, "I'll never go camping again!" I hear this a lot from women who were cold, wet, hungry, and miserable—and/or were in some kind of danger that hadn't been anticipated. Most often, they got into a bad situation because they tried to do more than they were ready for, or were talked into something without being given the appropriate support. (Or they went with a man who didn't understand that most women don't enjoy discomfort for its own sake.)

If you're a first-timer, either take a short trip with a low level of difficulty or go with a reputable guide. This reputable guide could be a friend, but be sure she has relevant experience and/or training, and that she's willing to take some responsibility for helping you.

If you choose to take a guided trip, be as discriminating as you would be in taking a new lover. Guides tend to exude confidence and expertise. This is a

Asking for It

There isn't a man in North America who hasn't been the butt of jokes about not asking for directions or help. Translate that to the backcountry as well. A Boy Scout leader once told me that he didn't worry too much about getting lost. Every time it happened, he brought the boys together and said, "Okay, now we're going to pretend we're lost, and you guys have to figure out how to get us home." So your choices are to ask plenty of questions before you go until you feel comfortable–or to take a troop of adolescent boys with you. My experience is that the former is more of a sure thing.

good thing, but make sure it's not egocentric bravado. Be direct and honest about your abilities and your concerns as a way of feeling out a potential guide. Ask questions about the guide's qualifications, previous experience, and expectations of you; also, ask for other women as references. If for any reason you feel as though your inexperience is being looked down upon or used to make you feel inferior, go elsewhere.

"Women as adventurers" is an emerging market. Virtually every backcountry trip-guiding company is offering women-only trips and excursions. Outward Bound and the National Outdoor Leadership School offer excellent, albeit expensive, guided programs.

If you can't afford a fancy guided trip, however, then go anyway! Begin with a stationary camp for a weekend. Or if you're really keen to get moving, then hike, ride a bike or horse, or paddle in to a site and then out again. Your best bet may be a short and not-too-challenging backpacking trip. Backpacking hones your lightweight camping skills and builds confidence in what you can do. You will be better at every other type of moving camp if you start by backpacking, but before you try even that, take a look at the following. And then prepare yourself for a good time.

Going Farther Afield

North America is a made for the backcountry camper, the wilderness explorer, the happy wanderer. The continent has been considered a cool place to explore since time immemorial. More recently, the wealth of untamed land in North America has created an ecotourism bonanza. The difficulty lies not in finding someplace to go but in choosing among a cornucopia of destinations.

Because many of the state, provincial, and national parks throughout the United States and Canada have become popular destinations for international tourists, you may need to reserve your space months in advance on some of the more spectacular routes. Start with the state and provincial parks. Most states and Canadian provinces offer an abundance of options. How to find them?

- The Internet has more information on back-country camping opportunities all the time.

- Check your local library and camping stores. Many books are available with information on great hikes, trails, and water routes near you. Local establishments will stock info that references routes in your area.

- Recreational camping and boating associations usually offer an extensive variety of books and route maps on paddling routes across the continent.

You will have a challenging enough time just living outside and carrying everything you need on your back. Don't multiply those challenges by facing a lot of unknowns. Think about safety concerns in advance, and don't introduce a lot of extra risk by not being prepared for where you're going and what you're doing. Most guidebooks will give you some idea of what's involved in a hiking route or canoeing trip. Always assume that the level of difficulty and the time allotments will be greatly underestimated. For some reason (hmm . . .) the experienced trippers who write these books often do not adjust down for the average tripper, much less the inexperienced.

Be Safe

When the trip is over, the storytelling begins. We tease our men for their fish stories, but what mother has not told her own childbirth stories with relish? The basics of a good story include action, surprise, and some element of danger or discomfort. And the whole point of telling the story is to make known how well or how humorously you managed the situation. Safely managing the risks of a camping trip will give you much reassurance and something to brag about.

The most important element of safety is planning ahead. Later in this book, I'll go into more detail about first aid and other safety considerations—but here's a quick look at some basics.

First Aid

When you choose to go into the backcountry, you should be aware that you are removing yourself from ready access to emergency medical services. This shouldn't be a problem, but you do want someone knowledgeable about first aid to be along with your group. Also, a need for minor first aid is no reason to interrupt a trip as long as you are prepared for it. A wilderness first-aid course can be an asset to you and your companions.

Hypothermia and dehydration are the most common health problems encountered in the backcountry—and both tend to sneak up on you. Get a good wilderness first-aid manual and read up on both conditions before you go so you'll recognize the symptoms and know how to deal with them before they become serious problems. And to avoid problems in the first place, just remember to drink plenty of water and never get wet (or stay wet for any length of time) when you're out in the backcountry.

Wildlife

Wildlife sightings are a treat, and it would be a shame if your group were always too noisy to experience them. You'll want to be especially careful of the larger animals, such as moose, or of carnivores like cougars, bears, and coyotes, but more often the wildlife that needs to be taken into account is the small kind—West Nile virus, ticks, poisonous spiders, snakes, and so on. In the woods, wear clothing to cover your skin and use insect repellent. If you keep shoes, socks, and a hat on, you'll be prepared for most problems.

As for the bigger animals, be wary of threatening them by your actions and proximity. We all have a personal space or safety zone around us, and we feel affronted if someone doesn't respect that distance. For an undomesticated species, that distance is—at a minimum—however far away you were when you first saw it. If an animal changes its behavior because of your presence, you're too close. Other safety tips are included later in this book.

If you have young children with you in an area that's home to carnivores, do not let them wander alone or on the fringes of the group; you don't want a predator misconstruing them as prey. You can deal with thieving small animals by keeping food packed up and cached when you're not cooking.

A checklist of safety issues that should be addressed can be found in appendix 3 at the end of this book.

2 Getting in **Gear**

So, girl, if you're still reading (even scanning), you're thinking, *I can do it, my way, feel good, and have fun—and maybe even pump myself up a notch in the eyes of a certain armchair skeptic . . .*

Believing you can do it is indeed the momentum you need to blaze your way into the backcountry. So harness that momentum and get going, because this kind of camping obliges you to investigate and plan thoroughly. You want to make sure the only impact you have is on your reputation.

Toward that end, read on to discover the specifics of what to carry, and why. Following these tips will make your travel more easy and enjoyable without sacrificing comfort and style at the campsite.

Get Organized

Organization of gear is always important to a group of women. (Though I must admit that while I love to pack things up, once I'm in the outdoors I become woefully undomesticated.) If you have enough of the right bags, sacks, buckets, and barrels, then there are sure to be group members who will rise to the bait and keep everything tidy and well organized.

I was once on a canoe trip that required a series of four short portages through small lakes and ponds. At the first portage, our group of eight women caught up to a group of men and boys on a fishing expedition. In order to pack and unpack their heavily loaded canoes, they had to get into the water, whereas we had everything on our backs and one or two olive barrels per canoe. It was easy for us to load and push off from the beach, and we were so lightly packed that we easily passed them. At the next portage, they caught up because we had stopped for a long break. As we were all getting into the water again, they wondered where all our stuff was and made a joke about our labeled food barrels.

At the final portage we were well ahead of them and moving out into the murky black pond when they approached the shore and went into the water with their first load. We were just saying good-bye when one of our group pulled a paddle up sideways and said, "Ye-eu! Leeches!"

Group Gear

When it comes to divvying up the group gear, make it a group activity. Bring it all together, pick out what you need and want, and divide it up. If one member of the group is unwilling to share her favorite gear, leave it behind if possible. It can be highly stressful (for *all* of you) to have someone's precious belongings with you on a camping expedition.

The more coordinated and cooperative your efforts are, the better your camping practices will be. Also, as I've noted, women have a tendency to bring along numerous "just-in-case" items. If you list and pack the group's gear together and agree to share everything, however, you won't end up with a lot of unnecessary duplication and weight.

After you've sorted the gear, it's time to pack it up for transport. Label barrels or make sure that containers are of different colors. Then everyone learns the organization system quickly and pitches in. Give in to your natural desire to have everything just so. If you camp with other women, you'll find that you'll always have some help in keeping it that way.

If you are carrying everything in your packs, putting the food into heavy-duty sealable plastic bags (freezer weight, not sandwich weight) is the way to go. Other items can go into packs with or without stuff sacks. If you *can* bring extra containers for the group gear, though, consider the following:

- Plastic olive barrels are airtight, lightweight, and great for carrying food on a canoeing, rafting, or kayaking trip. They can be acquired free from most Greek restaurants and a lot of delicatessens. You can purchase camping barrels, but they tend to be bigger and thus much heavier when full.

- You can purchase inexpensive screw-top lids for large plastic restaurant-supply buckets at most camping stores. These are a little heavier than the olive barrels, but the wider mouth will accommodate pots and dishes. They have a sturdy handle for carrying.

- Dry bags are waterproof bags in a variety of sizes (and weights) with an airtight roll-down top. Available at camping stores, they are good for tents and other "soft" items. They're good for food, as well—actually, they'll hold almost anything. When rolled, they have a sturdy carrying handle.

- Mesh bags and stuff sacks of varying sizes are available in camping stores. Drawstring bags are lightweight and good for organizing, but they don't "cushion." For items that you want to protect, such as stoves and pots, make breathable cloth bags from two waffle-weave dishcloths sewn on three sides with a drawstring closure on top.

■ Avoid using Rubbermaid and other plastic boxes or tubs, which cannot be securely sealed against animals or water. They are also cumbersome to carry when full.

Checklists for Everything; or, Time Management 101

Who hasn't learned the value of list making? Though there may be some women out there who enjoy the mental calisthenics of keeping track of details over a prolonged period of time, most of us don't. Make your own lists or use the ones provided in the back of this book. When you come home from a trip,

Uses for Garbage Bags

Take blue or orange, heavy-duty, garden-size bags. They won't tear as easily, and the bright colors will show up from a distance.

- Lining packs and stuff sacks.
- Dry bag.
- Pack cover.
- Groundsheet.
- Signaling device.
- Seat cover or tablecloth.
- Tarp.
- Sleeping bag in a survival situation.
- Raincoat.
- Water collector or carrier.
- Do-it-yourself shower—poke several holes in a bag full of sun-warmed water.
- Wound irrigator—poke a hole in a bag full of clean water.
- Bandaging.
- Garbage.

update your lists as necessary—you will have reduced your preparation time for the next trip by half.

If the man in your life tells you you're taking all the fun out of what's supposed to be a vacation, just remind him that ultimately there is no freedom without structure. See appendix 3 for checklists that will get you started.

Equipment Acumen

As a novice camper, don't go out and buy fancy, expensive equipment, and don't go buy what someone else tells you is necessary. Instead—to be as discerning as you need to be when shopping—go camping *first*. Rent or borrow as much as possible on your maiden voyage. Otherwise, it'll be just like those shoes in your closet that never quite fit but *oh-they-were-so-perfect*.

In the following pages, I have outlined some of the things you need to keep in mind when assessing the equipment you use or buy. You'll get many more opinions and insights from other campers: We are all experts. Just remember who it is you really have to please. . . .

Backpacks

When you first start tripping, you'll want to rent or borrow a backpack, but do make this one of the first pieces of equipment you invest in. A good pack for hiking or canoeing is essential gear. For kayaking, horseback riding, or biking, a good duffel bag or smaller packs that fit the mode of transport are better. Everything in your personal kit as well as some group gear and supplies should fit in or on the pack, and you should be able to carry it without difficulty.

Outfitters are finally making backpacks that are suitable for women. Because your center of gravity is lower, go for length in the pack, not width. The hip belt should sit atop your hips without constricting your diaphragm. The shoulder straps should rest lightly on your shoulders or, when tightened, just above your shoulders. This way, all the weight rests on your hips, and you can carry it without stress on your back as long as your stance is correct.

Your full pack should weigh thirty to forty pounds. There's no reason to carry more than that if you have prepared properly. When packing, try to put the heaviest gear, usually the food and kitchen, so that it sits at the small of your back. The next heaviest weight, such as tents, tarps, and Therm-a-Rest camping pads, are best at waist height. Attach your water to the outside of the pack between the hips and waist. Lighter weights like clothes and sleeping bag can go top and bottom. Make sure that outer layers of clothing are always reachable.

A bag that has openings at both the top and the bottom is the easiest to use. Try to memorize where you keep things in the bag, and always put things back where they belong. Use the backpack like a refrigerator. If everything is put back where it was found, then nothing gets lost and you know what you have.

Buying a Backpack

There are lots of interesting backpack features to choose from, which is why it's wise to rent or borrow one at first—you'll learn which of these features and benefits really suit your hiking style. When you do buy, get the best you can afford. This is one investment that will pay off in pack longevity (and maybe your own).

Before you go shopping, measure your back waist length from the bone that sticks out at the base of your neck to where the thinnest part of your waist is (or was, if you're pregnant). Then measure from your waist to the top of your hipbone. Add the two measurements together to get the optimum length of your pack frame. Most frames are adjustable—but don't compromise too much, especially if you're short-waisted. Make sure that your pack fits you comfortably and is not one cubic inch bigger than you absolutely need. Otherwise you'll be forever packing things you just don't need.

Sleeping Bags and Sleeping Pads

You'll need to be comfortable and warm when you're sleeping. Buy or borrow a sleeping bag that's down- or synthetic-filled. Do not use a flannel-lined, cotton-batting bag! They're heavy and bulky and will absorb moisture from your body and the air all night as you freeze.

Down bags are both lighter in weight and warmer. They're more durable in

Duct Tape

A maxim recently found its way around the Worldwide Web that said, "Duct tape is like 'The Force.' It has a dark side and a light side, and it holds the universe together." True enough, seasoned campers never venture out without a good supply of duct tape. It will stick to anything, repair everything, withstand any wear and tear, and last forever—so do not tape directly on skin. You can use it to bandage, brace, mend, patch, and reinforce anything, including broken bones, sprains, blisters, rainwear, shoes, tents, and canoes. The only thing it won't do is stick to a wet surface. Wrap a few feet of duct tape around your water bottle so that you always have some handy.

that they maintain their loft indefinitely, even though they compress better than synthetic bags. The downside is a higher price and the fact that they are cold if they get damp. A synthetic bag, on the other hand, is less expensive, washable, and warmer when damp.

Dampness can be minimized by the type of fabrics used in the inner and outer shell (covering) of the bag. All are breathable, but they offer varying weights and protection.

Buying a Sleeping Bag

When you buy a sleeping bag, shop around. Salespeople should be able to explain the differences in fills and fabrics in the outer shell. Decide which fill is best for you and your pocketbook. Don't get caught up in buying more than you need. It's easy to spend a lot of money on unnecessary high-tech options that will never make a difference to you if you camp only in warmer seasons.

You know best whether you sleep "hot" or "cold," so adjust the bag's temperature rating up or down by up to five degrees Fahrenheit to account for your metabolism and the climate you're likely to be camping in. A three-season bag is adaptable for most northern climates and can be converted to winter weight with the addition of an overbag or liner (which can also be used on its own as a lighter-weight summer bag).

Mummy styles are warmer, especially if your feet have a tendency to get cold—but climb in and make sure your feet will have enough room. While you're inside the bag, close your eyes and zip it up and down a few times to be sure the zipper doesn't catch on the fabric. (I have spent eight years cursing because I forgot about this test.) Tighten the top and then see how fast you can escape. You don't want to discover that you need the skills of Houdini to pee in the night. Finally, put the bag into its stuff sack and ensure that it will fit in your pack.

Sleeping Pads

An effective sleeping pad is lightweight and will insulate you from the cold and moisture in the ground. Insulation is more important than cushioning, but both are available to varying degrees in every sleeping pad.

Air mattresses, while comfortable, are heavy and have almost no insulation value. You also need to carry a pump or get light-headed every evening while blowing them up. Don't waste your money on one.

Closed-cell foam is a good insulator and is lightweight but can make for a hard night's sleep. A faraway friend and I still reminisce, whenever we're together, about a night spent with our "blue foamies" on a rock shelf with a view to die for. Our reminiscing must have sounded more like a lament when we got home from that trip because we both got Therm-a-Rests for Christmas that year.

The more expensive option is just that, a Therm-a-Rest self-inflating pad. This provides the best of all worlds. Many manufacturers now make pads comparable to the Therm-a-Rest; just be sure to get one with a durable outer covering that can be easily repaired on the trail. Most of them can be adapted for seating, an option that's well worth the extra few dollars if you can afford it.

Tents and Tarps

The first few times you sleep outdoors in a tent or under a tarp, prepare yourself to wake up at the crack of dawn. You have not known daybreak until you've heard it heralded by a choir of countless birds singing to a brilliant sunrise. It is impossible to convince a child that it's not morning yet, no matter the time, and the farther north you go in the summer months, the earlier it comes!

Sleeping out in the open, without a tent or a tarp for protection, is a fun experience—but not one that can be recommended in all locations or at all times of year. Your tent will be one of the biggest components of your backcountry getup, and one of the most important ones as well. Rain, sun, and bugs are just three of the reasons. On almost every backcountry trip, you'll carry a tent, a tarp, or both.

Tents for Rent

Though a cheap tarp will do until you can afford a better one, a cheap tent is a waste of money. As with your backpack, it's a good idea to use a few so you become familiar with your personal camping style and what you like and need in a tent.

Tarps

Carrying a tarp for rain, wind, or sun protection is always a good plan. The tarp can be used to protect a leaky tent or keep gear dry while tents go up or down in the rain. You can lay it on the ground to fold a tent on and keep it clean. A tarp can be made into a simple shelter so you don't have to bother with a tent if bugs and wind aren't an issue.

There are wonderful lightweight, versatile tarps available at camping stores—which can cost almost as much as a tent. A simple ripstop nylon tarp with a waterproof coating costs a bit less if you can make it yourself. Just be sure to ship-lap and waterproof the seams.

Despite their offensive colors, good automotive tarps are cheap and durable and come in a variety of sizes. They have reinforced grommets (holes) to tie ropes to in the corners and along the sides. They also come in varied weights, so choose the weight appropriate to your needs. Heavier tarps are more durable in freezing temperatures or in high winds.

Ultimately, however, a simple piece of plastic will do the trick—though you do need a way to attach ropes to it. You can effectively tie it up and prevent tears by bundling pebbles into the corners or sides: Put a pebble at the site where you'd like to attach a rope, and then tie the rope around the plastic, under the pebble, bundling it into a pocket. This will prevent the rope from slipping off the plastic, because as the rope pulls, it tightens around the pebble. Once it's done, it looks like a nipple (ouch!). I've recently seen some great positive-catch (meaning it tightens when pulled), heavy plastic alligator clips at a posh hardware store that will do the job, too.

Tents

The weight of your tent is in the fabric, poles, and pegs. Therefore you don't want any extra fabric for unused space in the tent. Most tents come with a fly—a protective covering that fits over the tent but up off the tent's surface. The lightest tents feature a lot of screening in the tent proper, which is great for hot-weather use without a fly, and for suitable ventilation in most weather with a good fly. Lightweight tents often look claustrophobic from the outside. Don't judge by appearances, though; instead, climb in with a friend (wear fresh socks and take your shoes off so you don't upset the merchant), then sit up and stretch your arms. Standing up in a tent is a frill you don't need and won't miss, ever, but you do want enough room to change clothes. Vestibules, created by a fly that is pegged away from the tent at a door, come in very handy and are often worth the little bit of extra fabric. See "Keeping Dry" in chapter 3 to find out just how handy.

Poles can be made of fiberglass, which is very durable, and what I use with teens or neophytes despite the extra weight. You can, however, get aluminum poles; these are much lighter, but they're also more expensive and can get bent with improper treatment. Tents supported by a single pole need to be pegged down. Titanium or aluminum pegs are lighter than a pole. So decide where this tent will be pitched. If it's on rock, you may want to use a free-standing pole arrangement and forgo the pegs when you can.

Once you've tried on a tent, cast a critical eye on how easy it's going to be to set up. Imagine the worst (*it is a dark and stormy night and you cannot find your headlamp and you really have to pee . . .*). A "cute" tent that has a tricky arrangement of poles fitting into long sleeves might not be worth the trouble or could get damaged on a bad night.

Also, find out about the warranty for your tent. Repairs should be provided at no cost to you, unless of course you have misused the tent. If there's going to be a lot of wear and tear on the floor of the tent from pitching on rough surfaces, you can protect it by cutting a footprint out of a lightweight plastic tarp. Just make sure that your footprint is slightly smaller than the floor of the tent and rests completely under the fly so that it doesn't allow water to run under the tent and pool.

Personal Items

When packing your personal items, don't plan on having clean clothes every day; a change of clothes for every two or three days should suffice. Refer to chapter 4, "Hygiene Hoodwinks," to see how that can be done without developing an "eau du backwoods" ripe enough to repel the bugs.

Everything in your personal kit should be unscented to avoid attracting insects and animals. Do not use fabric softener or dryer sheets that leave a scent on clothes or your sleeping bag. Do not put any food products in or near your pack and clothes. Keep gum, toothbrushes, and toothpaste in plastic. There are people who won't carry such items in their pack at all, and who change and air their clothes after cooking in them, but to me that's excessive. It isn't possible to hide from the bugs and bears; you just don't want to send out a boisterous invitation to supper.

Shelter from the Storm

A few good rules of thumb when buying a tent for protection from the elements are:

✓ For optimum weather protection, get a fly that reaches to the ground with at least 2 inches of space between the fly and the tent all around. Make sure the fly sits tautly on the tent and can be adjusted so it won't sag.

✓ Be sure you can see and feel the waterproof coating on the inside of the rain fly and floor.

✓ Make sure that there's plenty of ventilation, preferably on at least two sides and at the top.

✓ When the tent is pitched, be sure that the poles are secure enough in their pockets not to pop out in a wind.

✓ Look for a light color that will be cooler in warm weather and more cheery in dreary weather.

Fashion Sense

Staying warm, dry, and well fed will be of critical concern when planning your trek. There is no reason to suffer physical discomfort while camping, no matter what kind of weather the gods throw at you.

Understanding fabrics and their characteristics can help you layer appropriately and stay comfortable. Don't feel that you have to go out to buy high-tech camp clothing and personal gear. Many of your layers can be purchased in regular stores on sale or in used-clothing stores once you understand what you're looking for.

Characteristics of Fabrics

■ **Synthetic:** Composed of human-made fibers such as nylon or polyester.

■ **Breathable:** Will allow air to move through the clothing. This is a good thing, since sweat or moisture will not be trapped inside.

■ **Quick drying:** Will stick to your body when wet but will dry within minutes from the heat of your body.

■ **Water-resistant:** Will get wet, but water will not easily pass through. In a light mist or rain, the layers underneath will stay mostly dry.

■ **Water-repellent:** Will cause water to bead up and roll off. Water will not pass through—although it can eventually soak through depending on the amount of water, the age of the fabric, and the type of seams.

- **Waterproof:** Will keep the layers underneath completely dry. But remember that waterproofing sometimes comes at the price of breathability.

Types of Fabrics

- **Cotton:** Avoid cotton for camping. Cotton absorbs and holds moisture. Jeans are the worst: They'll stay wet for hours (days, if it's raining) and become very heavy. Cotton is breathable, and you can comfortably wear a cotton shirt if it isn't wet, or as a middle layer. Cotton canvas is water-repellent but will become heavy when wet. Cotton shrinks and will wrinkle if it's not blended with polyesters.

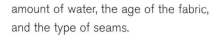

Uses for a Bandanna

- Sun protection.
- Headband.
- Wetted to cool forehead or neck.
- Washcloth or towel.
- Hankie or pee rag—make sure you have more than one with you if you use it for this!
- Sling.
- Bandage.
- Cold compress.
- Silt filter for water pump.
- Strainer.
- Pot holder.

- **Wool:** Wool is a great insulator. Wool and wool blends provide warmth and are breathable. Wool is water-repellent but can be heavy when wet. Wool shrinks. *Tip:* Because of their wool content, men's dress socks worn over synthetic socks (knee-high nylons) provide effective layers when hiking and are often less expensive than special hiking socks.

- **Nylon:** Nylon is lightweight, breathable, water-resistant, and durable; it also acts as a windbreak. It can be treated to make it even more waterproof. Nylon does not shrink and resists wrinkling. Gore-Tex, the most versatile outerwear in the realm, is made of specially treated nylon.

- **Polyester:** Polyester is lightweight, breathable, quick drying, and water-resistant—plus it has the ability to wick moisture away from the body. It can be less durable than nylon but has been engineered into an extremely versatile fabric. Polyester can be produced to mimic the qualities of silk as well as wool. It can be treated to become more waterproof. Polyester does not shrink or wrinkle.

Layering

In a perfect world, we would all have silk underwear. Mine would be in flashy colors, and my bras and briefs would match, sigh . . . When dressing in layers

Layer It on Me

When layering, remember these principles and you will always be comfortable:

- You are a hottie! (Your body is the heat source.)
- As in wine and humor, try to always be dry. (Wetness is the enemy.)
- Constant love outlives passion. (Keep your body temperature constant by adjusting your layers before you get too hot or too cold.)

for the outdoors, silk would be a good choice for all underwear, too, including long underwear. Polyester is a good alternative, and any synthetic is better than cotton. Winter or summer, it's best if moisture is wicked away from your skin and dried quickly.

The next layers should provide comfort and/or warmth if needed. Quick-drying synthetic shirts and pants are good for summer hiking or paddling. If warmth is required, a polyester fleece or wool layer will provide good insulation. This is where a cotton layer may fit in, because multiple layers insulate better by creating air spaces. If there's a cold wind, then a nylon windshell will seal in the warmth generated by your body. If it's wet out, you'll need head-to-toe waterproofing. The more synthetics you use, the more compact and lightweight your clothing will be.

3 Weathering the Weather

I f you're looking for a way to slow down the sands of time, take a camping trip in the rain. Sure, you can always go home in bad weather, but that's cowardly—and besides, sometimes home is a long way away. A camping trip is like buying a lottery ticket: After you've invested in it, giving up just isn't an option; the lottery isn't over until all the numbers are drawn. When the weather goes sour, prepare yourself for prolonged bad weather, and then whatever you get will be an improvement.

This chapter covers some basic weather forecasting info, but more importantly it contains information on how to stay warm, dry, and comfortable when conditions are bad. Fair-weather-only campers may be missing the point and not learning some of Mother Nature's best lessons. Camping provides a way to occasionally reacquaint ourselves with the natural environment—and what's a more integral part of our natural environment than the weather?

Of course, there are certain situations where you should take extra precautions or get out of the backcountry and back to safety. Whenever there is the possibility of sudden extreme environmental or weather conditions—hurricanes, tornadoes, flash floods, fires—beat feet. There are also some very high risks associated with bad weather and wet or cold campers with no opportunity to get dry and warm. If anyone's health or safety is threatened, either by the probability of hypothermia occurring or by sudden extreme environmental conditions, do not hesitate to pack up and go home.

Weather Forecasting

There are weather radios that will work in the backcountry and can be helpful in letting you know what's coming your way. They're a particularly good idea if you are boating. Though they are expensive, you may be able to rent one. That said, there's nothing more reliable than knowing how to interpret the sky and the atmospheric conditions to get an up-to-date weather report.

Weather Wisdom

These bits of weather lore come from age-old observations of atmospheric conditions and are remarkably reliable in helping you predict the weather:

- When there is a ring around the moon, bad weather is on the way.
- Red sky at night, sailors delight. Red sky in the morning, sailors take warning.
- When there is dew on the grass, rain will never come to pass.
- When grass is dry at morning light, look for rain before the night.
- Birds flying low or unusual rodent activity during the day means bad weather is on the way.
- When the smoke of your campfire swirls or is beaten down, rain is on the way.
- When someone says it "smells" like rain, it's because the scent of vegetation is more distinctive before a rain.

Everyone Knows It's Windy

Wind is the most immediate predictor of weather, since it always accompanies changing atmospheric conditions. A sudden rising wind or a change in the direction of the wind can portend a sudden change in the weather—as well as the onslaught of evil in old movies.

Generally, wind from the east brings storms, and wind from the north brings cold. Of course, this is less reliable if you're in a mountain valley, where the wind could be funneled in odd directions. Then you'll need to figure out what the wind is telling you from temperature change.

Watch the Clouds

Clear skies or high clouds usually accompany fair weather. The clouds that hang lower in the sky are the ones that will bring bad weather. Still, big fluffy clouds can bring storms if they become bunched up and are many-headed, or if they're dark and menacing. Fluffed-up clouds can also change quickly, so you want to keep an eye on them just as you would a cat that was fluffed up—most of the time it means nothing, but things could get nasty. A benign exception is white fluffy clouds out by themselves over the ocean, which can simply indicate a landmass beneath. Low dark blankets of cloud bring rain or drizzle. These will move through more slowly than fluffy clouds, which can move very fast—just like that cat—and must be watched more carefully.

Keeping Dry

Staying warm and dry in wet weather becomes a real challenge, but with a little good sense and some care, it *can* be done. The primary rule to follow is:

Keep wet things away from dry things and out of the tent.

Do not bring wet rain gear, clothes, or hiking boots into your tent, because you will increase the humidity and condensation in the tent, and everything will become damp. It'll be like living inside a steam bath, only a lot colder. A tent may have to come down and go up wet, but the exterior will dry out quickly with a few minutes of breeze or sun as long as you haven't filled it with wet belongings. If you go through several days of rain, this becomes a challenge, but it is absolutely necessary. When you have packed everything in individual bags, however, the process is a lot easier.

Port in a Storm

Always have a way to shelter your entire group in inclement weather. When I'm traveling with a group of women, I try to take one tent that's large enough for the entire group to sit in together. Eight to ten women can sit in an empty six-person dome tent and avail themselves of shelter, warmth, protection from insects, and a social opportunity. Just be sure that the tent's occupants agree to host the group when their tent is chosen. Since you should not cook or eat in a tent, bringing a party tent does not preclude the need for a tarp. When forced to make a choice, take a tarp and leave the large tent at home.

The Zen of Tarps

I once read a magazine article called "The Zen of Tarps." The phrase has stuck with me because it exactly describes both the construction and the use of sheltering with a tarp. A tarp can provide sun protection, rain protection, or windbreak. It can be used to keep gear dry while you set up a site; it can protect a leaky tent; it can even become a tent if needed.

When pitching a tarp, have lots of strong polyester cord that won't stretch too much and isn't affected by moisture. You will want to situate your tarp with respect to the environment: It doesn't need a center prop or angles for sun protection, for instance, whereas in the rain it needs both. A center prop for a

Bug Attack **TIP**

Do not use bug repellent in or around your tent: It will break down the waterproofing qualities of the fabric. If you've been invaded by bugs, cut 6 inches of duct tape and 6 inches of string. Fold the duct tape over the center of the string about 1 inch from one end so that 5 inches of sticky tape is free. Sprinkle a little sugar on the sticky tape and hang the strip in your tent to catch that pesky mosquito or fly. In the morning, you can use it as a silent valet to clean the dirt out of the tent corners.

An Easy-Tie Knot

If you're looking to tie up anything to a pole, tree, or thwart that will ultimately need to be untied, the handiest knot is the round-turn with two half hitches. Use it to tie up your boat, gear, or clothesline. Start by wrapping the rope twice around the pole, tree, or thwart. At this point, you can tighten it if necessary. Tie the first half of a regular knot with the loose rope end to the taut rope. This is a half hitch. Tie it again, only this time just loop the rope without pulling it all the way through. The knot will tighten the more it's pulled on–but when it's time to undo it, just tug the rope end, and it will unravel.

tarp can most easily be made by tying a rope up high across the center, and underneath the tarp to create a ridge. For use as a wind-break, the tarp needs to be firmly tied along its length in a vertical position against the wind. This is where the Zen comes in. You will need to assess the site, the environmental factors, your needs, and the size of the tarp so that your creation is unique, intuitive, and functional.

Keeping Toasty

When it's very cold at bedtime, people instinctively tend to bundle up in all their warmest clothing, zip the tent up tight, and climb into their sleeping bag. Yet this is the recipe for frigid sleep. Think instead of arranging your sleeping ensemble into a layering system that includes your body, the bag, and the tent.

Your sleeping bag is like an envelope of warm air, with your body as the heat source. Lightweight pajamas or underwear are all you need to wear—or ought to wear: If you pack clothes around your body, the envelope becomes cold, and so will you. Wear nothing if it suits you, because in this case less is more. If it's cold, synthetic long underwear is as much as you'll want to wear. You can always add a warm hat and a pair of lightweight wool or fleece socks!

You must also do a proper job of insulating underneath you. Any good dense foam or Therm-a-Rest–type sleeping pad will do the trick. Do not use

Dry Boot Tips

To keep your boots dry at night, nest one inside the other in a dry spot inside the vestibule of your tent. You can also nest your boots by putting one inside the other so they are not open to the air and put them in a bag. Placing a crushed sprig of cedar or fir inside them will keep the odor from knocking your socks off when you go to put them on the next day.

If you don't have a vestibule, try making "boot buddies": Pound two sticks upright into the ground just outside your tent. Hang the boots upside down on the sticks and put a plastic bag over each one. Tuck the shoelaces inside the boots, and make sure the sticks are long enough that the boots don't touch the ground.

an air mattress; they're heavy, bulky, and provide poor insulation.

Add insulation using fleece clothes or a reflector blanket underneath the trunk of your body, since cold more readily seeps into the bag through the ground than via the air above. You can zip your coat around the bottom of the bag to add insulation around your lower legs and feet.

Moisture = cold. The tent is your windbreak and waterproofing layer and needs to breathe. It should be well ventilated with the windows partly opened, no matter what the outside temperature is. There is a lot of moisture in your breath. If you close up a tent too efficiently, it can actually rain inside because of condensation.

Tarp Tip

Rainy weather is a great time to set up a tarp with the tents situated so that all of their doors open under the tarp. Then you can remove all your wet things before entering. Many sites don't offer enough space to do this, so bringing along a large umbrella for all to share can be handy. (An umbrella can also be used as a sail and an anchor if you're boating.)

Campfire or Not?

Ah, the lure of the campfire. Romantic light flickering over the campsite, the crackle of the logs as they burn down while you settle in for the night, song sessions as you sit on logs around the glow, and s'mores.

The Downside

Despite the romance associated with long evenings around flickering flames, campfires are unreliable in bad weather, too hot in hot weather, and ecologically unsound. When we gather fuel for a campfire, we are removing habitat and hiding places for small animals and insects as well as brush, which would

Cozy Bag Tips

- Avoid the urge to make your bed as soon as the tent is up, because the bag may become cold and damp. If you have allowed your body or the bag to get cold before bed, you can warm the bag with a hot-water bottle (try to figure out two uses for that!) or rocks heated in the fire and then wrapped in foil.
- Keep your bag waterproof during the day by storing it in a stuff sack lined with a plastic bag. You can air it in the sunshine, but otherwise put it in its sack soon after you get up, when the bag is still warm. Don't open it again until you're ready to climb in at night.
- When you're tucked into your sleeping bag, try not to burrow in so that you're breathing into it; this would increase the moisture content inside the bag.
- Finally, bring the next day's clothes into the bag with you, and you'll be a happy camper in the morning.

Make Your Own Firestarters

- Candle kisses: Finally, a use for all those candle ends! Take a 1- to 2-inch piece of candle and roll it in a 4-inch square piece of waxed paper. Twist the ends like a candy wrap. Lights easily and burns well.
- No-yolk cakes: Take a fiberboard egg carton and fill the cups with dryer lint or sawdust. Pour melted paraffin in each cup, and when it hardens, break them apart. Wax can be messy, so melt the paraffin in an old can set inside a pot of boiling water. Bend the can into a spout and pour while the egg carton sits on a section of newspaper—which you can also use to start a fire. These work great but are heavier to carry.
- Survival starters: Take five or six cotton balls and coat them generously in petroleum jelly. Stuff them into a film container. These are lightweight and compact but will not burn as long.Pot holder

otherwise break down eventually to become food for the trees.

Some parks will provide you with firewood from their forest management programs, but you should go camping always prepared never to need a fire.

Cooking over a campfire is more romantic than it is practical and should only be planned with that in mind. I likewise plan flexible menus that can be rearranged for weather concerns and are easy enough to be executed by anyone. If the recipe is tricky, include the directions in or on the package—you never know who will end up doing the cooking.

Minimum-Impact Fires

You may decide to have a fire for reasons of warmth or to burn garbage, particularly sanitary items or food refuse. If you do, pick your spot well. If you spot evidence of a previous fire circle, use it as long as it's sited away from trees. The best spot for a fire is on mineral soil (sand or gravel)—if you build a fire directly on the ground, nothing will grow there for several years. You can carry a sheet of heavy-duty aluminum foil, doubled thickness, to place on loose sand or gravel and build your fire on it. Be sure that the fire cannot spread and is far enough away from trees and large rocks, which can singe and be defaced or damaged.

A fire for warmth should include some hardwood or ash so that you create plenty of coals to generate heat. A fire to burn garbage should be very hot with lots of flame, so use plenty of dry kindling, pine, and softwood. When the

TIP

Testing the Heat

To test the heat of a fire for cooking, hold your hand over the fire above where you will be cooking and count aloud slowly: "One . . . two . . . three . . ." Keep going until you have to pull away. Anything less than six is a very hot fire and is good for boiling water or toasting. From six to ten is a medium fire; you can cook on it. Baking is best at eight to twelve.

fire has died, pour water or sand over it until there is no more smoke. When it has cooled, take all pieces of unburned garbage with you, scatter the charcoal and ashes, and remove all traces of the fire.

Lighting Your Fire

Fires need oxygen as well as fuel to ignite and burn. When you lay the wood for a fire, start with small pieces, and place them so that air can circulate around them. Laying some of the wood in a four-sided log cabin arrangement with a tepee either outside of it, or in the center, works well.

A good firestarter can be a lifesaver when the wood is damp. It's unsafe and often ineffective to use stove fuel to light a fire. When everything is wet and you need dry tinder to start a fire, remember that the dead branches around the base of an evergreen are drier than the tinder on the ground. It will not hurt the tree as long as the branch is dead enough to snap off easily. These branches have been referred to in the past by the politically incorrect term *squaw wood*; it just goes to show you that women have always had a practical approach to bush life. Like our Native predecessors, be sure to have at least two ways to ignite your fire. Three is better.

4 Hygiene
Hoodwinks

Is it possible to keep yourself comfortable and relatively clean on a back-country trip? Actually, you'll find that being out in the fresh air continuously airs you out and keeps body odors down. Daily washing dries out your skin (wrinkles!) or hair (dull and lifeless!), so this is a good opportunity to learn to do without. Bathing every third or fourth day should be sufficient.

A Wash on the Wild Side

Cleanliness is important, but when it comes at the expense of the environment, how much is enough? That is the conundrum of camping hygiene. This issue may present the most difficult choices for women in the backcountry. Both in their kitchens and with their personal hygiene, women tend to be fussy.

Daily bathing and hair washing, clean clothes every day, brushing after every meal, and makeup just don't fit in with minimum-impact camping. It's really all a matter of perspective, however, because you *can* keep clean and look fine without damage to a wilderness environment, as long as you're willing to compromise.

Before we get to other ways of keeping clean, a note about bathing: Never introduce soap into freshwater sources even if it is biodegradable, and always dispose of gray water (wash water) in an environmentally sound way. This means that bathing in the lake with soap or shampoo isn't in the cards, and water use must be kept to a minimum to avoid copious quantities of gray water needing disposal.

Gray water can be properly disposed of in a latrine. If there is no latrine, then it must be strained and scattered at least one hundred paces away from the site or a water source. To strain the water, you can use a Handi-Wipe or other similar disposable porous cloth, which you can then put in with your food garbage. Or you can poke holes in the bottom of a used plastic bag with a

Instead of a Shower . . .

Here are some good ideas for staying clean while minimizing water use:

✓ Take along unscented baby wipes. You can sponge-bathe with one when you get dressed or use one after a swim.

✓ To bathe, take a swim and then sponge-bathe with a few drops of camp suds or a tiny bit of biodegradable soap, using a pail to rinse. Dispose of the gray water properly.

✓ Use a bandanna, not a washcloth. Washcloths soak up soap, leaving less for you, but a bandanna will give it all to you and then provide you with a better rinse.

✓ To clean your hair, thoroughly wet your head and your bandanna. Put a few drops of camp suds or a tiny bit of biodegradable soap on the bandanna and lather it up. Use the bandanna to scrub your scalp. Don't worry about the hair. Rinse your head in a bucket. It won't take much water to rinse but you'll be amazed at how clean your hair feels. Conscientiously dispose of the gray water.

✓ Hang your clothes in the sun or a breeze, and they'll smell fresh and clean in a short time. Quick-drying clothes rinse clean with no soap and dry fast, so take at least one set and you'll never run out of clothes.

✓ Brush your teeth with a cup of water. Put about half the usual amount of toothpaste on a dry toothbrush and brush your teeth. When you're finished, take a big swig of water and swish. While you are swishing, rinse the brush in the remaining water. Spit into the cup and faithfully dispose of the gray water.

✓ If you have to brush after every meal, learn how to "dry brush." Put a tiny drop of toothpaste or none at all on a dry toothbrush and brush your teeth. When you're finished, take a big swig of water, swish it around, and swallow. It only seems gross the first time, and it works.

fork and put a little bit of grass in the bottom over the holes—but then you have to dispose of the bag and the grass with your food garbage. Scattering the water means pouring it on the ground, but not in a quantity that will pool in any one place.

The Joys of a Cat Hole

I once watched a National Outdoor Leadership teacher of zero-impact ethics wave a bandanna at a group of seventy-five teenage girls while explaining that she kept it in her pocket and wiped herself with it when she was out in the woods. As she put it back in her pocket, the girls recovered from their shock and got grossed out in unison. Teenage girls have a way of getting to the heart of a matter without pretension, and then, sometimes, with nothing but.

What the instructor meant—and what was lost on the fragile sensibilities of the teenagers—was that pee is basically clean. She was not using the bandanna for other bodily wastes, or for anything else. The truth is that you can pee anywhere as long as you don't have any infections. This is obviously something that men and cats have innately known for years.

It is only necessary to dig a cat hole to defecate. Although digging a small hole for hygienic decomposition is most common, there are environments where it's more ecologically sound to pack out feces. In the Southwest, smearing them on a rock to dry out and blow away is appropriate. In ocean environments, it's considered acceptable to bury waste in a shallow hole (1 or 2 inches) well below the high-tide line. In crowded marine areas, however, it's better to use a pail with some seawater in it that can be taken offshore and dumped in the deep water. Most established sites offer a latrine, so the need to dig or pack or smear at all is rare. You probably won't have thought this much about the topic since you were two years old. . . .

Digging the Hole

To dig a cat hole, find a spot just off a trail and at least one hundred paces (200 feet) away from the campsite or water. In some places, digging is a challenge, so look for soil that has a good amount of organic and decaying material on top, such as under a leafy tree. With a spade, remove any surface growth (say, mosses or grasses) in a mat along with its roots. Move it to the side and store it upside down (or root-side up) where it won't be damaged. Dig down at least 6 inches (more for a bigger group), trying not to cut any large roots as you go. The hole should not be more than 10 to 12 inches in diameter. Put all the soil in a pile next to the hole. Find a sturdy stick on the ground and stand it in the soil. Mark the spot with fluorescent trail tape tied up high so that it can be easily found.

Covering Your Tracks

When you use the hole, scoop a little soil and/or organic debris over your business and stir it with the stick every time. This will mix in the bacteria and microorganisms that aid in decomposition, hastening the process. Put your toilet tissue and sanitary items in a bag. When the hole is filled to 2 inches below the surface, replace the rest of the soil and the turf. Press it down firmly with your foot. Yes, it is a bit squishy and revolting. Remove the bag and the trail tape and move on to the next spot.

Or Try This

If you are somewhere that's extremely dry, or cold, or there's no organic debris, then you shouldn't dig a cat hole. In an environment that doesn't lend itself easily to decomposition, you will need to pack out your human waste. This can be done by making a container, often referred to as a "poop tube," from black PVC pipe with a screw top at both ends to scoop the stuff into; you can also use a covered pail with a plastic bag liner. Other options, including chemical toilets, are available at camping stores.

If the previous instructions have discouraged you from camping altogether, take heart: Much of the wilderness lends itself to ready decomposition. But if you really don't want to pack out waste, avoid glacier, desert, and permafrost areas. Also, most regularly used sites have latrines, so you won't need a cat hole. You'll only have to dig while you're on the move.

5 Eating Well

Eating well on the trail can make the difference between a so-so trip and a great one. Without good, nutritious, lightweight food options, the best hike into the wilderness can turn into a disastrous, uncomfortable experience. Meal planning for a challenging camping trip should include a balanced diet with a high nutritional content. The combination of continuous physical activity, stress from the metabolic demands associated with living outdoors, and the good old fresh-air factor requires a nourishing menu. This chapter will give you some tips for preparing food before your trip and while you're on the trail. Recipes are included in appendix 1.

Your Portable Kitchen

Every good cook knows that there's more to good food than just a recipe: The recipe is simply a list of the ingredients that must be coaxed carefully into a delectable meal. It's also necessary to have the right tools and to know how to use them. The efficient lightweight kitchen compares to haiku poetry: It is compact and focused in its use, and yet there is a lot of flexibility in its interpretation.

Of course, a lot also depends on the kind of food you carry along on the trail. Canoeists and others who don't carry all their food on their back can take the food and camp kitchen in buckets and barrels. This chapter will show you how to pack delicious, nutritious food in as few pounds as possible.

Free Pot Sets

When I first started backpacking, I used aluminum cans (and a pot lifter) for my pots and a tin pie plate as a lid. I bent a spout into one of the cans and called it a kettle. They were lightweight and worked well enough until I could afford a good pot set. If you decide to try this, use sturdy cans that have no lining and are manufactured in North America. Don't try to fry in them; it doesn't work.

A Lightweight Kitchen in a Bucket

This kitchen will fit in a five-gallon bucket with a screw-top lid attached (lids for restaurant-supply buckets can be bought at camping or farm-supply stores). Store the fuel separately. Put the kitchen into mesh bags or dishcloth bags so that everything can be kept clean and hung up to dry or store when it's not in the bucket.

Utensil Bag

4 sturdy chopsticks—1 will stir, 2 are tongs, 3 make a whisk, and 1 will surely be lost.

Lightweight plastic 1-cup measure with a handle that can also act a ladle.

Pot gripper—available in camping stores instead of mitts or
pot holders, which can get wet and are then ineffective.

1 sturdy plastic fork.

Small sharp paring knife.

Small plastic cutting surface—a 6-by-8-inch piece of a plastic place mat will do the
trick.

Can opener, if you take cans—a thumb-sized model is available in camping stores.

Small plastic (T-Fal) egg lifter—if you're frying or baking
in a pan.

Dish Bag

Bring enough sturdy, lightweight plastic bowls, spoons, and cups for everyone. That way, they nest compactly and can be carried with the kitchen. You can buy them at a discount store, or just use margarine tubs and have everyone bring a spoon and a small plastic mug.

Dishwashing Bag

I use an open mesh nylon bag for this since everything in it is usually wet.

Small bottle of biodegradable liquid soap.

Handi-Wipe cut into smaller cloths for washing and straining.

Small plastic pot scraper or piece of abrasive pad. Sand also works well, if available.

8- to 10-inch square of chamois—to dry things before nesting them when it's time to
pack up.

Pots

1 pot that will hold the one-pot meals for the size of the group.

Lid for the large pot that can double as a frying pan.

1 pot for desserts, extras, or water, with a lid.

1 kettle (optional).

Trail Nutrition

A backcountry trip is not a good time to be dieting. Eat as much as you like since you'll be expending plenty of energy on your trek in the wilderness. In addition, the colder it gets, the more calories you will use in staying warm. You can eat commercial food if you're determined to diet, since the servings are small and the taste can be disappointing. But if you really want to take care of yourself, make your own food before you go. Don't carry too many "empty calories" such as candy or cereal products that aren't whole grain. They're just weight with no purpose. A variety of fruits, vegetables, grains, legumes, nuts, and seeds will boost the nutritional content of recipes.

About Weight—in Your Pack

Years ago, when I was a naive camper, the heritage and romance of "bannock making" had me intimidated. I believed that my version, which consisted of mixing Tea-Bisk or Bisquick with milk to make a stiff dough and then toasting it on the end of a peeled green stick, was a rudimentary interpretation; I needed to learn the true "art" of the bannock.

As a result, I signed up for a session on bannock making offered by a local man who was reported to be an expert on camp food. Bob began by expounding on the benefits of making bannock. His rationale for bringing plenty of bannock along on a canoe trip included the need to introduce fresh hot bread into a boring camp diet. This sounded right to me; dehydrated food can certainly sometimes use the boost that a good bannock provides. I waited eagerly for some "secret" recipes that would complement certain dishes.

Bob was a burly guy with a full beard and mustache and a soft, low quality to his gravelly voice. As he spoke, I envisioned him cooking a camp breakfast that would include strong coffee and a melt-in-your-mouth bannock with warm honey and cinnamon on it. I could tell by looking at him that I wanted his recipe; it was destined to be good.

We were all going to cook some bannock, but first Bob wondered if there were any questions. A young man near the front questioned whether lots of bannock wouldn't weigh you down, and did Bob know what the relative weight of his recipe was per serving compared to other dehydrated options?

Bob became very thoughtful, and I was awed by the astuteness of the question. Why hadn't I wondered about that? After what seemed like a long time, Bob answered that he was a canoeist. Though that seemed to make sense to a few folks, some of us had clearly retained a look of puzzlement, so Bob went on to say that compared to all the cans and coolers in the bottom of his canoe, the box of biscuit mix was pretty lightweight.

Bob's bannock turned out to be pretty good because it (and he) was hot.

But while Bob may have been burly enough to paddle extra weight and waste in and out of the backcountry, dinner out of a can isn't worth the effort. Paring down the weight for a moving camp is essential. And dehydrated foods are the way to go for a lightweight minimum-impact camp, but not just because they're compact and weigh less. Dehydrated food also has fewer odors in both storage and preparation, so it's less likely to attract animals, and easier to stow and store. With dehydrated foods, the food preparation is minimal—so the kitchen can be lighter weight as well. In addition, rehydration can be done prior to cooking; less fuel is needed.

You can roll into camp and have a meal ready within the hour without any work beyond getting fresh water and lighting a stove. You'll look like a superwoman when you produce a gourmet meal in less than an hour from a self-sealing bag.

Food Preparation

One or two hours before serving a trail meal, cover with water the dry ingredients that need to be rehydrated. Double-bag them in freezer-weight zipper-locking bags. This will reduce cooking time and save fuel. For convenience, carry a two-cup bottle of purified water to use for rehydrating the supper.

Early rehydration also helps ensure different consistencies and flavors in the recipe. If you try to cook it all at one time without rehydrating, some ingredients are likely to turn to mush. Properly dehydrated food is not susceptible to bacterial growth, but as soon as the food rehydrates, it is. The cooler you can keep it, the better, so don't store it in the sun or next to your body. Once you have started the process of rehydrating, cook the food within two hours.

Stove Sensibilities

Good cooks have an innate sense of how flexible the timing and speed of cooking can be without over- or undercooking the food. This skill includes understanding the way your stove heats and how well your pots distribute heat. When you take cooking outdoors, you also need to take into account the effects of air temperature, wind, and elevation on heating the food.

Just as every kitchen stove is different, so is every single-burner lightweight stove. Get to know your stove (and how to repair it) before you go camping. Propane-and-butane-mix stoves simmer better than white gas (naphtha). They require you to carry canisters of gas, however, and the propane ones cannot be recycled. White gas stoves are a little trickier to use, but the fuel is inexpensive, and the containers can be refilled easily.

If you don't have a stove that simmers foods well, try diffusing the heat with a tin pie plate under the pot, creating an air space or double-boiler-type space. Windscreens and pot adapters come in very handy to regulate the heat under the pot. They can help keep your cooking from being affected by wind and cold. Get a lightweight version or—at the very least—take some heavy-duty aluminum foil to wrap around the outside of the stove and pot to keep things steadily heating. If all else fails and you have the time, you can bring everything to a hard boil, insulate the pot well with foil and warm clothes, and wait an hour.

Gourmet Presentations

Picnic tables are not ordinarily available on backcountry sites. You'll find yourselves eating perched on logs, on rocks, or on the ground. Consider it ambience, but be prepared with something dry to put under your butt if the need arises. It doesn't lend anything to a meal if it's served to people who are all standing around.

Presentation can be half the enjoyment of any meal. Many of the recipes in this book have garnishes—or you can improvise! For special occasions or when the food needs to be an extra morale booster, bring some tea lights and

Staples to Go

The recipes in this book are self-contained and don't need additional flavorings. Still, sometimes a dish just doesn't go right, and you need a little food first aid. Try this:

- Use instant mashed potatoes to thicken a watery sauce.
- Bring a saltshaker for the 20 percent of women who aren't going to suffer from hypertension in old age and the ones in the other 80 percent who don't care.
- For those folks who need to liven things up, take a shaker of all-purpose savory seasoning consisting of one tablespoon each of paprika, garlic powder, and powdered parsley; one-half teaspoon each of pepper and mustard powder; and one-eighth teaspoon of cayenne.
- For the sweet-oholics, take a shaker of all-purpose sweet seasoning consisting of three tablespoons of sugar, one tablespoon of cinnamon, one-half teaspoon each of nutmeg and ginger, and one-quarter teaspoon of cloves. You can also use instant hot chocolate as a flavoring on a dessert or breakfast.
- Ketchup, jam, and honey in tubes or small plastic jars might help you get rid of leftovers.

Wild edibles are a wonderful and idyllic way to dress up or garnish a dehydrated menu. Still, there are a few things to remember if you'd like to try some:

✓ Never pick wild plants unless there's an abundance, and then be sure to pick a little from many plants. Do not pick enough to upset the ecosystem or destroy a plant.

✓ Positive identification is a must. It can take years to learn plants well enough to make a positive identification. If you aren't a naturalist, stick with learning a few plants well. Pick ones that are common, easy to identify, and don't have a similar poisonous cousin. Try sorrel, mint, dandelion, watercress, violet, strawberry, and the onion family.

✓ Take a good field guide with you to double-check identification.

✓ Avoid mushrooms and nondescript berries unless you are trained specifically to identify them!

pick a wild bouquet, or garnish the plates with natural objets d'art from a pine tree or nonpoisonous wild plant. Shake the bugs out first!

Water Purification

Okay, now some bad news: The pristine condition of North American fresh water is threatened. Assume that all aboveground water sources contain both bacteria and waterborne parasites. Viruses are not a problem for us yet. Still, there was a time within the past few years when parasitic contamination was not a concern in many places. It is now. Any water purification process that does not address parasites is not safe. Chlorine and halzone are therefore questionable; iodine works but tastes bad.

Following are the most pleasant and effective methods for purifying water, along with some of their advantages and disadvantages:

■ Boiling at a rolling boil for one full minute: This is only convenient at mealtime, uses fuel, and requires time for the water to cool if you want it for anything other than cooking or hot drinks. It's cheap (good filters and tablets are not), however, and you can still have pure water in the event the filter clogs or a bear steals your pack with the tablets.

■ A water filtration system with a 0.02-micron filter: Filtered water is good for supplementing cooking, washing, and drinking water. Filtering water is the most expedient method—the water can be then used immediately. Still, filters can clog or break, and you must be careful not to cross-contaminate the outflow with the intake.

- Chlorine dioxide chemical treatment: This requires a container and twenty minutes. It's good for filling water bottles and getting water while traveling.

Each of these methods, used according to directions, will retain a good water flavor and deal with any harmful organisms in the water. Camping stores are full of products for water purification, so when you go shopping, ensure that these standards are met. Your best bet is to keep your bases covered and use all three methods when you go on a trip.

Meal Cleanup

When it comes time to clean up, be sure all food and food waste are properly stored or disposed of. Do not rinse dishes directly in a water source. Food should never be allowed to pollute a water source; rinsed dishes can be a source of bacterial growth and waterborne parasites. Do not put leftover food in a cat hole or fire pit—eat it, or pack it up and take it out.

You can prerinse dishes with unpurified water, but then the water you use will need to be filtered and disposed of as gray water, and the dishes will require proper washing. You'll want to use purified water. You can boil it, but then you'll either have to wait until it cools or add cold filtered water. You can wash dishes directly in the ocean, but use a clean-water rinse.

It's easiest to wash the dishes in the cooking pots. If you have a collapsible washbasin, you can use that, but I prefer to use the washbasin for personal hygiene and do the dishes in my pots.

6 Safety and First Aid

Early on in my outdoor experience, I talked some women into coming camping with me because I liked them and enjoyed their company. It wasn't a moving camp, and I was newly exploring camp cooking: I had planned a weekend full of gourmet cooking over the campfire. We had to drive quite a distance to get to the site in south-central Ontario, which was private property and pleasantly remote. Everything was going to be great.

We got up on Saturday morning in late October to eighty-five-degree-Fahrenheit weather. The heat and humidity were oppressive and promised only to get hotter. One of my friends was six months' pregnant and could not get up from under the tree that was shading her. Another spent the morning organizing everything on the site and then became sick with heat exhaustion. Every bit of food that I had brought required cooking, and I had not brought a stove. I had to light a fire and build it up for every meal.

I had never been so hot in my life as when I tended that fire. I have since enjoyed an August in Florida and menopausal flushes, both of which can compare. As I prepared delectable hot herbed tomato soup with mini cheese dumplings for lunch, I had the sinking feeling that my menu was going to destroy me. True to my premonition, when I pulled a pot with a faulty handle off the fire, the boiling soup splashed on me. I had thought that I was going to the woods, but I had actually ended up in hell. Worse yet, I was only halfway through my excellent menu.

Not to mention, I realized I had some serious second-degree burns. I looked around me and quickly assessed the situation. We were at least an hour from a hospital, maybe more. We had no telephone or other means of communication. I was the driver and the only person with any first-aid or camping experience. If one of the other women *was* able to drive me to the hospital, I would be leaving the group abandoned. Two were already feeling ill, and some others started to get panicky when they saw me.

Safety Support Kit

Safety support or survival packs are fun to create for folks who like working on crafts and puzzles. You have to find ingenious ways of packing multiuse items into the smallest possible space. Still, your pack won't help you if you don't have it with you when you get lost; you must commit to carrying it.

I was able to quickly get some cold water on the burns and then some ice from the coolers to cover them and ease the pain. I soon went into shock and made the decision, based on the fact that no one would be able to execute my elaborate menu, to stay put and self-treat. Duh . . .

We all know that accidents happen, even with good preparation. This chapter will consider how to manage the unexpected and turn it into a "good story." It starts with a knowledge of basic first aid. After that, you'll need to understand how to be a good risk manager, including knowing how to coexist with the other critters in the woods. Finally, you'll want a few survival skills, just in case.

The best piece of safety advice is to avoid situations that put you in peril in the first place. If your preparation has been good, you've already done 90 percent of that work, because you know what the dangers could be and have accounted for them. It's a bit like safe sex: Once you've taken the precautions, it's all fun, unless of course there's an "accident." Refer to the "Preparedness Checkup" in appendix 3 to see how well you've prepared.

Basic First Aid—What to Know Before You Go

Always check on and treat health problems as soon as they surface out in the backcountry. There is no profit in being brave about your health issues, unless you aspire to martyrdom. Everyone else in the group will be endangered by your foolishness if you go that route. Following are some basics to take into consideration when dealing with first aid in the wilds.

Ailments

Women no longer suffer from the vapors and hysteria or die of broken hearts, thank God, but they do get sick, and sometimes they have the bad luck of getting ill on a trip. The ailments that you are distinctly at risk for on a backcountry expedition are dehydration, heat exhaustion, and hypothermia. After that, I would have to list stomach problems due to a changing water source or diet; reactions to insect bites; and exposure to new allergens.

Remember that first aid is not meant to be diagnosis and treatment unless you have no other choice. Treatment suggestions should be used in non-invasive-to-invasive order to avoid overreacting to a problem, which can be just

Sick and Tired in the Woods: Symptoms and How to Treat Them

Stomach Problems

Symptoms of appendicitis: Persistent abdominal pain (with or without nausea, vomiting, diarrhea, or fever) should be considered suspected appendicitis until you rule it out. Assess recent bowel movements, ovulation discomfort, or any injury that may be causing the pain.

Treatment of possible appendicitis:

1. No food or fluid.
2. Rest; keep warm and quiet.
3. Evacuate—assistance is required immediately.

Treatment for stomach upset:

1. Make sure the person is warm and dry.
2. Encourage rest; help the patient relax; offer herbal tea (mint or ginger is best).
3. If constipated, adjust the diet and ensure a good fluid intake. For heartburn, offer antacid. For queasiness or nausea, offer an antinauseant. For menstrual pain, offer an analgesic.

Treatment for vomiting:

1. Give nothing by mouth or try clear fluids only until the vomiting stops.
2. When it has stopped, use rehydration salts.
3. If blood appears in the vomit or if it's not controlled in twenty-four hours, seek medical assistance.

Treatment for diarrhea:

1. Proper and frequent hand washing by everyone is essential.
2. If several people have similar symptoms, boil all cooking and eating equipment for five minutes and check your method of purification for all drinking and washing water.
3. Give clear fluids only for twenty-four hours. If it's not controlled in twenty-four hours, obtain medical assistance.
4. If symptoms persist, use an antidiarrheal and rehydration salts. If there is fever, pain, or blood in the feces, do not medicate; obtain medical assistance.

Allergic Reactions

Symptoms of mild allergic reaction: Sneezing, runny nose, itching watery eyes, rash.

Treatment:

1. Topical—soothing lotion.

(Continued)

2. Topical—hydrocortisone cream.
3. Oral—only if symptoms are very troublesome—give antihistamine.

Symptoms of severe allergic reaction: Tightening in the throat; hives; agitation; a sense of fear, foreboding, or apprehension; itching; swelling in the mouth, lips, or tongue; breathing difficulties; wheezing; chest tightness; asthma attack; abdominal pain; vomiting or nausea; dizziness; pallor; sweating; collapse. Not all symptoms may be present. If the problem is not treated, a sensitive individual may progress to the life-threatening condition of anaphylactic shock.

Treatment:

1. Give antihistamines as soon as symptoms appear.
2. Administer epinephrine (adrenaline) in EpiPen or Ana-Kit form. Those with known serious allergies usually carry antihistamines and epinephrine with them to administer by injection, but they may require assistance.
3. Evacuate—assistance is required immediately.
4. If medical assistance is not immediate, administer antihistamines every hour and repeat the epinephrine when necessary to a total of three doses.
5. Maintain the airway and administer CPR if necessary.

Symptoms of skin rashes or exposure to poisonous plants: Itching, redness, rash, fever, headache.

Treatment:

1. Remove contaminants as soon as possible.
2. Lightly wash the skin with soap and water or rubbing alcohol; rinse well.
3. Do not rub or scratch the skin—a dry dressing may help.
4. Apply a soothing lotion or baking soda and cool compresses.
5. If the problem persists, apply hydrocortisone cream.

Altitude Sickness

Symptoms: Diffuse (all-over) headache and constant, unusual fatigue for the activity, lightheadedness, shortness of breath, appetite loss, nausea, sleeplessness, facial swelling, swelling in the extremities.

Treatment:

1. Stop your ascent and rest.
2. Descend if symptoms do not improve within one hour.
3. Administer an analgesic (acetaminophen).
4. If symptoms become worse or there is any coughing and cyanosis (blue skin color), descend immediately and obtain medical assistance.

Bites and Stings

1. Allow some bleeding, to cleanse the wound.
2. Clean with soap and water.
3. Apply topical antiseptic and topical antibiotic.
4. Apply a sterile bandage.
5. Record the species of animal and whether the animal provoked the encounter.
6. Obtain medical assistance if there is any danger of rabies or tetanus.

Treatment for bee, wasp, or hornet stings:

1. Have the person sit still for at least twenty minutes.
2. Remove the bee stinger carefully and quickly by brushing it out with a cotton ball or tissue.
3. Use baking soda and cold compresses or an ice pack to relieve pain and local swelling.
4. If symptoms of an allergic reaction are evident, give antihistamine.
5. Continue to observe for symptoms of a severe allergic reaction for four hours.

Treatment for insect and spider bites:

1. Rest, cold compresses, soothing lotion such as aloe vera or baking soda. Do not use anesthetic cream (those with *-caine* in the list of ingredients).
2. Observe for symptoms of an allergic reaction and treat accordingly.
3. Hydrocortisone cream may be used only if symptoms persist.
4. If you suspect a poisonous spider bite, seek medical assistance. If possible, take the dead spider with you.

Dehydration

Symptoms: Headache, muscle cramps, light-headedness, fatigue, clumsiness, irritability, dark-colored urine during the daytime.

Treatment:

1. Slowly but continuously drink several liters of water so as not to urinate it out.
2. Avoid caffeinated beverages.
3. For severe dehydration, use rehydration salts.

Heat Exhaustion or Heatstroke

Symptoms: Headache, nausea, dizziness, rapid pulse, profuse sweating, chills, pale skin, fainting, delirium.

(Continued)

Treatment:

1. Rest in the shade.
2. Remove clothing; wet the skin with cool water.
3. Drink fluids; use rehydration salts.
4. If delirium, unconsciousness, or convulsions occur, rapidly cool the person by any means available and obtain medical assistance.

Hypothermia

Symptoms: Shivering, mumbling, uncharacteristic behavior, confusion, disorientation, muscle cramps, uncoordinated movement, stiffness, cold and pale blue-gray skin.

Treatment:

1. Stop further heat loss by providing shelter and removing any wet clothes.
2. Insulate and warm the person, covering her head with a warm hat.
3. Give warm, sweet liquids.
4. If shivering has stopped, apply warmth to the trunk of the body by any means available and obtain medical assistance.

Toothache

Symptoms: An abscess will present throbbing pain; the gum may be inflamed. A lost filling will cause sensitivity, sharp pain, and discomfort.

Treatment:

1. Apply a cold compress on an abscess.
2. Make a temporary filling with absorbent cotton and clean wax.
3. Offer an analgesic for pain.

Wounds and Infections

Treatment:

1. Keep open wounds clean by always using potable (filtered or boiled) water to wash the wound and the skin around it and by applying clean or sterile dressings (bandages) to the wound. Open wounds should be covered for twenty-four to forty-eight hours.
2. Apply topical antibiotic.
3. Soak in hot salt water or a baking soda solution.
4. Monitor the person's temperature. If it seems elevated, if radiating redness is observed on the skin, or if tenderness is noted in any glands, obtain medical assistance.

as troublesome as not reacting to it. Bring someone along who knows how to monitor ABCs (and not the kindergarten kind), give CPR, and treat for shock. And remember, if symptoms persist or become serious, get help!.

Medication

Play a game of true confessions before you go, with everyone sharing personal health concerns and noting any regular medications she takes. This is worth recording and putting into your first-aid kit, along with health insurance information, since it is information that will be requested if there is a need for emergency medical assistance. If anyone may require special emergency assistance because of medical conditions such as asthma, diabetes, or severe allergies, everyone should be versed in dealing with them.

An Emergency Compass

To use your analog watch as a compass, lay it on a flat surface. Hold a matchstick on the watch's center to create a shadow that you can use to line up the hour hand so that the hour hand is pointing toward the sun and making a straight line across the watch with the shadow. The point on the watch that is halfway between the hour hand and twelve o'clock (one o'clock during Daylight Saving Time) will be south.

Your first-aid kit should contain over-the-counter medications for the group, but check the dosage information on the packaging of all medications and record it if it's removed from the package before going into the kit. *Never* exceed recommended dosages, and closely monitor anyone who is medicated: The medication could interfere with her strength, stamina, or level of awareness (something that you wouldn't necessarily notice at home, but may be a safety issue in the backcountry).

Always treat with as little medication as possible. Medication can mask symptoms that can provide the clues to more effective treatments (for example, a headache caused by dehydration). At home, getting rid of symptoms is safe because you can always get to a doctor, but in the backcountry, it's better to figure out what's causing them and treat the cause. Only use medications if it's necessary to keep the group moving.

Finally, the one prescription medication that I carry is epinephrine. I had a close call with someone who unexpectedly went into anaphylactic shock as a result of a wasp sting. Only the administration of megadoses of antihistamines got her safely to the hospital, which mercifully was not that far away. Allergies and allergic reactions are becoming more common all the time because of environmental degradation. Because a first reaction is unpredictable, I keep an EpiPen in my first-aid kit. You'll need to talk a doctor into giving you the prescription, but most of them will understand the need if you explain.

How to Think on Your Feet

Just as important as being prepared is being flexible. When things go wrong, you need to be able to calmly assess the situation and create a plan that may bear no resemblance to your original. And the same goes for when people are having a good time and things are going well—the old adage, "If it ain't broke, don't fix it," holds true. Here are some tips for dealing with the unexpected.

Planning Ahead

I have found that some women feel more secure if everything is spelled out and "under control." Be sure that everyone is knowledgeable and prepared. Good organization, planning, and communication are necessary elements in good risk management. But too much resistance to changing plans is just not safe. When we plan too rigidly, then we don't leave ourselves enough flexibility to change the plans when problems occur. So even though it's a good thing to plan ahead and prepare, always keep it in the back of your mind that things can change. Plan like a CEO . . . but once you get out there, go with the flow.

Confidence and Safety

There is a lot to be said for adopting a confident attitude in a tricky situation even if you don't feel particularly confident. The "Whistle a Happy Tune" mentality will win the day more often than not. Staying calm is a fundamental step in managing safety. Some risks we can assess beforehand, and those are easy to plan for and safely manage. But sometimes risky things happen without our expecting them. That's when the safety is "in your head." Our ability to respond directly and effectively to reduce the risk or to safely manage it can make all the difference in the outcome. Plan for the worst and expect the best.

Assessing Risks

When we reassure ourselves that a situation will right itself or we "make do" too many times, we create unsafe environments. We may get away with it—but that's luck, and not to be counted on.

When I burned myself with hot soup at a camp where I had taken all my noncamping friends on the hottest weekend of the year, I put everyone in a precarious situation. Tragedies in the backcountry almost always occur because of a series of faulty decisions, none of which seems like a big deal. The erroneous steps that time were:

1. We hadn't given any thought to how remote we were—after all, it was "just a weekend," and we had driven in. We ended up in a remote area,

Survival Skills

The British Royal Air Force (RAF) tests your ability to survive by asking you to prioritize the contents of a survival kit. A few years ago, I was assigned to a group of men and women who were asked to do just that as a team-building exercise. Because I had a reputation as an outdoorsperson and can be a forceful leader, I was given free rein by the team. I focused on making sure everyone was going to get fed and have their wounds dressed . . . and as a result, we were all lost at (simulated) sea. We didn't do much team building. What I should have done (I now know) is remember that survival is the *top* priority. If you get totally lost, stay put and use every means to signal for help first. You can *then* secure your health and safety and get comfortable.

As soon as you realize that you are lost, stop and go no farther. A great program for kids called "Hug A Tree" teaches them to find a tree to stay with and hug if they ever get lost. Grown-ups should do the same—although if you know for sure that you can get to a nearby beach or clearing, go there to hug your tree. Figure out the best ways of signaling for help and set yourself up to systematically do so. Light a fire if it's safe, and fly or drape brightly colored plastic where it can be seen. Blow your whistle or air horn every ten to fifteen minutes. If you see any aircraft or boats, use glass or a mirror to signal if possible. If you're lucky enough to have flares (a must on the ocean, and a good idea in any boat), use the biggest one immediately. After the initial flare, save any others until you have reason to believe that a search effort is within the flares' range, or your situation becomes dire. Flares have their own science, so learn about them before you go.

Next, you'll want to secure your health and safety. Ensure that you are warm and dry and can stay that way even if the weather changes. Tend to any wounds and create some shelter, using whatever is at hand. You'll be amazed at how strong dental floss is, for instance. A makeshift sleeping bag can be made from a lawn-and-garden garbage bag lined with a space blanket. You won't be able to stretch out, but it works.

If possible, secure a water supply and start rationing it a little at a time. Lick the morning dew off smooth leaves—don't worry, it's all good. Collect rainwater. Ration whatever food you have in the same way, eating and drinking tiny bits only when you can't go on without something.

Appendix 3 includes a checklist detailing a "Safety Support Kit" that will help you do all of the above—and it's easy to make. Take it with you and learn from my mistakes. The next time I'm going to help a group survive and I feel like nurturing, I'll hug a tree!

far away from emergency medical services, without knowing.

2. My plans were rigid and not flexible enough to deal with the circumstances that presented themselves.

3. There was no one else in the group who had enough experience or knowledge to take over the decision making when the need arose—and no one else was able to respond directly and effectively to address the risk.

4. Shock is a life-threatening situation, and no one but myself was aware of this. Typical of shock victims, I was not thinking rationally.

5. We were all embracing denial because that "felt better" to us.

Handling Emergencies with Resolve

Once you have received the input and opinions of the group and/or have decided on a reasonable course of action, do not second-guess or waiver. Further discussion or arguments will be counterproductive and will undermine successful outcomes. Go with your decision and do not change your mind(s). Resolve and a positive attitude are your most important survival skills.

Wildlife Wisdom

One of the best parts of wilderness camping is the opportunity to observe wildlife. It's important to remember, however, that the animals *are* wild and as such should be observed only from a distance and as unobtrusively as possible. Many critters can become dangerous if they feel threatened, but most are respectful of you if you are respectful of them.

If you find yourself engaged in an unpleasant encounter with a wild animal, the following information will serve you well, even if it's not a bear. Whether it's a bear, moose, cougar, or raccoon, understanding the animal's modus operandi and remembering to keep your actions calm and deliberate will help you out of some tricky situations. Parks have an obligation to warn you of the presence of possibly dangerous wild animals, and most do offer pamphlets and education about those animals. Be sure to access the information and learn what you can before you head out.

Bear Aware!

The good news is that bears are making a comeback in North America. The bad news is that North Americans have forgotten how to coexist with wild animals in our environment. Bears have a terrifying reputation, and much of it is undeserved. There are many myths about bears that just aren't true.

- **Myth: Bears are predatory animals.** Unless bears have been fed by people and thus habituated, they will usually steadfastly avoid people. Noise is frequently enough to drive them away. Sometimes a bear may become hungry or sick, from loss of food supply, illness, old age, or loss of teeth, and then it can be threatening and aggressive. This is rare, and in areas where the bear population is monitored, those bears whose behavior becomes threatening are destroyed as soon as it is detected. The only other reason that a bear will threaten you is if it feels that you're threatening it—perhaps you've inadvertently cut it off from its cub or its food supply. Noise and staying observant will help keep you out of those situations, as well.

- **Myth: Bears are nocturnal.** Bears are biurnal. The time to look out for them is in the morning and in the late afternoon and evening, not the middle of the night.

- **Myth: Bears are attracted to menstruating women.** There is no evidence to support this theory whatsoever. Bears *can* be attracted to strong odors from food, food scraps, and garbage. If you use minimum-impact practices regarding food and sanitation, you shouldn't attract bears. The smelly campers are the ones who fry bacon, meats, and fish, dumping the scraps and grease in the water, fire pit, or latrine. Your period will never

Bear Cache Rope on a Pulley

Use a sturdy rope that doesn't have a lot of stretch to it and is smooth enough to slide easily. Thirty feet of ½-inch polyester rope works well. Permanently tie a large pulley to one end.
- Find a strong branch at least 12 feet up or higher and toss the pulley over the branch. For more ballast, you can tie a full water bottle to the rope at the pulley end.
- Feed the rope over the branch by lobbing the rope upward until the pulley comes down to you. Put the other end of the rope through the pulley.
- Holding the rope by its free end and by its middle, slide the pulley back up to the branch.
- Pull enough of the free end of the rope through the pulley to tie on a bag that is on the ground.
- Take the middle loop of rope that's left and tie it securely to the tree trunk. The cached bag can now be pulled up to the pulley, and the new slack rope tied again to the tree.

produce that kind of "come-hither" scent for anyone, including bears.

■ **Myth: Bear bells and pepper spray attract bears.** We've all heard the stories of bears being called to bells and liking the taste of pepper spray. I have only ever heard these stories from people who were actually trying to defend their right to shoot and kill a bear with a gun. Government agencies, biologists, and conservation authorities all agree that noise is an effective deterrent and that pepper spray, when used correctly, will repel an attacking bear *(Backpacker Magazine,* September 2000). There are also other effective means of repelling an attacking bear, such as loud popguns and flares. Whatever means you choose to use in bear country, be sure that everyone in your group knows how to use it, as well as knowing about the dangers of an accidental discharge.

■ **Myth: If you see a bear, get away as fast as you can.** When dealing with an approaching bear, do not turn and run. This may trigger an aggressive response in the animal. Instead, hold your ground while talking loudly to the bear and getting the attention of your companions. This may be enough to discourage the bear. If it doesn't, then you will need to decide if you are talking to a grizzly bear. A grizzly has a long snout like a German shepherd. Brown and black bears have flatter snouts and look more like the classic stuffed animal. Do not identify the bear by color, which is unreliable as a species indicator. If it is a grizzly, don't look in its eyes, keep talking, and slowly back away, stopping if that causes the bear to approach. With a black or brown bear, you can be more aggressive: Get up on a log, wave branches and your arms, yell, and look at it.

If someone arrives with the bear deterrent or you have it yourself, do not use it unless the bear attacks. If the bear feels outnumbered, it may retreat. If the deterrent is spray, check the wind direction and decide who has the safest opportunity to spray it into the bear's path. If you don't have deterrent and the bear attacks, throw a pack or similar object to distract it. If all else fails, lie facedown and spread-eagle on the ground, covering the back of your neck with your hands. This way you cannot be flipped over, and all your vital organs are protected. The bear may abandon you after some sniffing and pawing.

Remember that wild animal attacks are unusual. Like fights with your spouse, they are most often the result of miscommunication and misunderstanding. Cache all your food and keep your site clean, and you shouldn't have any uninvited guests. Many parks in bear country provide caches, but be prepared to cache in a tree at a primitive site or an unexpected stopover.

7 The Art of Happy Camping

The Bruce Trail in Ontario runs the length of the Niagara Escarpment. The trail was clearly laid for the purpose of challenging the hiker, since it runs up and down the escarpment in a zigzag. The result is comparable to a mountain hike—in a relatively flat province. Our group of six was backpacking the Niagara peninsula end of the trail in the July heat and humidity. The shade in the woods provided little relief, because it was offset by the loss of the breeze. We had become cunning at shaving weight off everything that went into our packs, but as we hiked along with a "mere" thirty-five pounds on our backs, we were understandably cranky. Complaining about the illogic of running up and down the side of the escarpment for no apparent reason, we came to the conclusion that it must have been a man who'd broken the trail. Commiseration while unreasonably blaming half of the human population when you're irritable is another advantage of camping with women.

As we entered a clearing at the top of the escarpment, we saw the backsides of some kids running away from a small brushfire that they had just started. We gathered around the fire and began discussing the best way to smother it before it got any bigger. From behind us on the trail came a solo hiker. He entered the clearing, took one look at the fire, and emptied his entire water bottle on it. In the ensuing conversation with the undeniably handsome hero, we learned that he was completing a six-week-long backpack of the length of the trail. He had started with a friend, but the two had parted company and were now leapfrogging each other along the way. Our hero was sure that he would beat his buddy and therefore wasted no more time chatting with us. We had a refreshing drink from our own water bottles and then each splashed a few drops on the charred spot to alleviate our guilt as we went on our way.

At lunchtime, we found a shale rock face in the center of a slow-moving creek. We were relieved to have come upon a water source before encountering our hero again, this time prostrate with dehydration or heat exhaustion. We shed our hiking boots and waded in the cool water. We set up our kitchen, prepared an excellent meal of cashew wraps, filtered and drank the fresh water, and were resting on our packs when the hero's buddy came through. He ate an energy bar and was on his way. As we sat there musing about their feat and admiring their stamina, we couldn't help but wonder why, given the choice, they would travel alone—and competitively. None of us could conceive of a reason to go it alone, although most of us knew men who had done so. How could it be fun? We decided it must be a "guy thing" *(but damn, sure makes for a nice body on a guy)*. We packed up our lunch things satiated, revived, and pleased with our company.

We had a long afternoon hike, but after a while the heat seemed bearable, and the packs became just so much more body weight. Pretty soon we were all giggling at everything that was said . . . *everything*. Now *this* was camping, we decided. Girl style.

Group Fun

Go girl! You've decided to venture forth, and you're as ready as anyone can be—or so you think. This is when the real work begins, and the real fun starts. If getting prepared was like dating, this is managing the wedding and honeymoon. You're gonna love it, but there's a fair bit of follow-through required to create memories worth remembering.

Fun and Games

The most successful outdoor adventures for women contain two essential elements: a mutually supportive group dynamic and plenty of good food. Sure, we love our safety, comfort, sleep, humor, and wine—but these two factors are what will make or break a trip for women. If these core qualities are present on a backcountry trip, then any other hardship unfolds into the challenges that become part of the trip lore. The food is the easy part (see appendix 1). A positive group dynamic takes a concerted effort.

Mental health professionals agree women's ability to laugh and cry, as well as their good verbal communication skills, contribute to their well-being. Laughing, like crying, provides a cathartic release; we feel much better after a good one. It also requires recovery time, however, and you may need to be flexible with your plans to accommodate for it. No matter; there's nothing like a good break!

Recent research into the effects of hormones on the brain has found significant evidence that women's brains are wired for talk, multitasking, and interaction, whereas men are more often wired to be single-minded and focused. As with all sex-related differences, there are more differences

Musketeer Morale

Never lose sight of the fact that it must be "all for one, and one for all." Following are some guidelines for keeping a positive and supportive group dynamic going.

- ✓ Determine beforehand who's in charge of what. Having no decision maker is just as bad as having too many. Everyone in the group should acknowledge and endorse the division of leadership before you go.

- ✓ Decide how decision making will occur. Group decisions are best unless you are in crisis. Consensus isn't usually difficult with a group of women, but you may need to agree on a democratic process.

- ✓ Share your expectations. Discuss what you're hoping to enjoy/experience before you go. You may be able to facilitate each other's goals, or you may find that you need to compromise on your own.

- ✓ Define your roles. Some of you may dislike certain jobs while others enjoy them. Some people like to be told what to do, while others are organizers. Discuss your roles and responsibilities, and keep the discussion open throughout your adventure. We all change our minds.

- ✓ Plan for fun. Don't plan to bust butt if everyone isn't interested. Add-on hikes or activities should be optional. Plan for downtime and fun activities. Have a group hair wash or foot soak. Bring jokes and group treats.

- ✓ Stir the pot. Unless you are a previously cohesive group, it's best to mix yourselves up a bit. Pairing up or grouping yourselves for the duration of the trip can be boring or, worse, stressful and unpleasant. Mix well and let friendships develop among everyone.

- ✓ Be aware of the strength of your chain. A chain is only as strong as its weakest link. Be considerate of the well-being of every member of the group. You'll find that you all have your moments.

- ✓ Evaluate as you go. Take time to discuss how things are going and what can go better. Allow fickle behavior to spice up the discussion and create some laughs.

If you're going to make it through the long haul, keep track of each other. When the going gets tough, pace yourselves only slightly faster than the slowest person. When you take a break, allow enough time for a real rest. A three-minute gulp-and-go is fine, but if that's the only break, it just won't do it. You'll need enough time to feel refreshed—but not so much time that you get stiff or sore. Try for five to fifteen minutes.

The exception will be toward the end of an overly long day if everyone is getting tired; slow the pace considerably, but don't stop for more than a gulp-and-go. Tired people are more at risk. Stopping may feel too much like quitting for their bodies, so it's better to keep moving lest they stiffen up and become accident-prone. Conversely, speeding up will also aggravate mishaps. When people are tired, take your time and arrive at your site safely.

Finger Clock

To estimate the time to sunset, hold your hands at arm's length, palms facing you so that your fingers line up under the sun, parallel to the horizon. Each finger (not including the thumb) that will fit between the sun and the horizon counts for fifteen minutes. Therefore, two fingers are thirty minutes; six are an hour and a half.

between individuals than between sexes, but most of us enjoy a periodic respite or pause and don't need to be talked into taking a break.

Drinking

There are lots of good reasons to take regular breaks, but a fundamental one is to drink. When working or playing outdoors, everyone should carry a large water bottle with plenty of fresh water in it. To prepare for activity, it's a great idea to hydrate in advance. Drink lots in the days before you go out.

The ways in which we normally lose necessary water from our bodies and become dehydrated are by urination, perspiration, and aspiration (exhaling). Water loss from the first two is obvious, but aspiration is usually less well understood. We continually exhale warm moist air, evidenced by the cloud that we see when we exhale in cold weather. There are two ways that aspiration can create enough moisture loss to dehydrate us. The first is through heavy breathing, as when we are exercising; this is sometimes compounded with moisture loss from perspiration. The second is when the outside air is extremely dry, so that we're taking in dry air but aspirating or exhaling moisture.

In any type of weather, therefore, it's essential to drink during activity. We can lose from two cups to two quarts of water every hour if we are exercising, no matter what the temperature is. If the fluids aren't replaced, we'll quickly feel the effects of dehydration, which can include headache, muscle cramps, light-headedness, fatigue, clumsiness, and irritability. Since all of these symptoms are easy to misinterpret, make it a habit to check your companions' (and your own) water intake at the first complaint. Once you are feeling thirsty, you may have already depleted your body's water stores by as much as one-third. Also, if your urine color during the day is darker than a pale straw-colored yellow, you may be dehydrated—but be aware that some foods and vitamins can also darken your urine.

Snack!

Plan your breaks ahead of time, as they will provide a short-term goal and break up the activity, particularly if it is strenuous, into manageable segments. We all find working more productive if we can measure our progress. Set up your breaks as rewards for progress: "As soon as we get to this point on the map, we'll stop for a break." Remember to replace the salt that is associated

Keep Hydrating

The Leakproof Bottle

Pop-top-style bottles are not leakproof. Good lightweight leakproof bottles can be obtained by reusing spring water bottles that have a firm screw cap. Or try a brew-your-own-beer bottle.

Winter Water

In winter, keep a leakproof water bottle inside your coat so that the water is readily available and doesn't freeze. At night, if it could freeze, put the bottle in the sleeping bag with you.

Drinking like a Fish?

Small amounts of water drunk often as you exercise will help to keep you from losing fluids through urination. "Camel-back" water bottles that will allow you to continue exercising while you drink are great.

Sweet Talk

For those who don't like to drink plain water, dropping a Jolly Rancher candy in the water bottle every time it's filled will flavor the water pleasantly; even if it gets warm, it will still be palatable. You can also add drink crystals or powder to the water, but really sweet drinks are not as thirst quenching. The powdered drink crystals may also color the bottle and leave a flavor in it.

with moisture loss from perspiration and urination with a salty snack. Then introduce variety into the snack menu. A different candy, fruit leather, bars, or interesting dried fruit will make the necessary salty trail mix a lot less boring.

Enjoy the Downtime

It's always worthwhile to learn the lore of the area where you will be trekking. There are many such books available at outdoor stores; if you can't find one about the area in which you'll be traveling, you can also try contacting a local library or local tourist information center. Identifying plants, birds, and interesting geology, as well as sharing the stories of the trail, can break up the monotony of a trip. I have also used other books with pithy short pieces for a read-aloud "story time," resulting in much enjoyment for the group. This is the one case in which the extra weight for a single-use luxury is worth it. The right book can broaden your experiences and help you share quiet enjoyment or a spiritual moment with your fellow travelers.

In the Cards

You'll need some activities for your downtimes. A deck of cards is the lightweight solution to what to do if it rains or you're windbound. A card game that creates jovial competition can amuse a group for hours. See appendix 2 for some ideas.

It's an Art

Sometimes fun ambushes you—everyone feels playful and responds to it—but those moments are rare. Most of the time we have to make our fun, and it is an art. It starts with each group member feeling that her needs are being met or at least being heard. After that, it's a matter of seizing the moment! As grown-ups we may forget this skill as we seek validation and credibility in a competitive society. If you are going to have fun, don't allow Type A behavior to rule the day—turn it into a joke. I have confiscated watches and come up with awards to recognize inane priorities in the backcountry: the Martha Stewart Award for Excessive Perfectionism, the Wendy Darling Award for Excessive Nurturing, the Susanna Moodie Award for Excessive Complaining. Humor that is not hurtful can diffuse a "people problem" better than anything I know; it will go a long way toward creating the necessary mutually supportive group dynamic. Now all you need is the food. . . .

Epilogue: Leaving Susanna Behind

When my husband and I talk about the people whom we admire, we always say, "I'd love to have so-and-so to dinner." Many folks whom we discuss are smart, interesting, or controversial, but the true test of whether we admire people is whether we want to share a meal with them. I'll often go so far as to imagine what I'd serve to them.

I wouldn't, for instance, want to have Susanna Moodie to dinner. As interesting as I think she is and as much as I empathize with her, I couldn't concoct a meal for her, and I don't think I'd want her around for long. There is a woman mountaineer, however, who would be on the top of my list: Phyllis Munday (1894–1990).

Phyllis Munday explored, photographed, and mapped British Columbia's coastal mountain peaks. She was a remarkable naturalist, conservationist, and environmental teacher. She saved lives; she named mountains; she was the first woman to climb Mount Robson, the highest peak in the Canadian Rockies. She was used to carrying packs, chock-full of her homemade camping equipment, which weighed three times as much as the pack I'm used to carrying. I like to believe that I can do almost anything, but I'm sure I couldn't do half of what Phyllis did. Maybe I could pack sixty pounds, bushwhacking and climbing 30 hard miles to set up a base camp, but she would carry up to three such loads.

"My soul belongs to all the mountains, for this is heaven. Thank God, he made me like this," wrote Phyllis in her diary.

So Susanna may be our evil twin, but the alter ego that we are going to nourish once we get out in the wild will be like Phyllis. Or like some other woman whom we now discover had remarkable, courageous, and productive adventures in the wild.

Our mothers and grandmothers did many things that were never recognized or noted as the bold and adventurous accomplishments that they were.

As Ann Richards, former governor of Texas, noted, "Ginger Rogers did everything that Fred Astaire did, but backwards and in high heels." And all the while it was Fred's feet that got showcased, while Ginger's pretty face and dress were his props. If gender is an obstacle to our ability to face the challenges of the great outdoors, then it's only because we have lost touch with the feats of the women who settled this vast continent. Working harder for less recognition is our legacy—but not our sentence.

It doesn't have to take as much raw courage or brute strength to get us where we want to go if we define our participation. We do not have to accept the roles and expectations that are assigned to us. Mother Nature is a woman! Our horizons now are in redefining how things can be done. It's time we made sure that there are no barriers to anything women choose to do. See ya in the woods. . . .

Appendix 1:

Pack-and-Go Trail Recipes

L et's face it, any food is a comfort when you're tired, hungry, and away
from home—but good food is essential to a truly successful camping trip.
A well-executed gourmet meal at camp can make everything seem very
fine indeed. Add the sweet smell of the woods and the satisfying taste of ful-
fillment and friends and you have it all.

These pack-and-go trail recipes are one-pot meals unless polenta or bannock accompanies them. All require early rehydration of some ingredients.
Most of the recipes cook in ten to twenty minutes and need to be watched
and stirred. All will benefit if you let the pot sit, covered, for ten to fifteen minutes after they've finished cooking. If it's cold outside, put a fleece over the
pot to retain the heat.

Quantities and measurements in each recipe may differ with different
brands of store-bought ingredients. Always check the package instructions for
items such as instant mashed potatoes, powdered broth, powdered eggs, and
instant milk, modifying the recipe if necessary. The following recipes provide
four servings, each slightly larger than a commercial serving size—for four people with healthy appetites. Still, the measurements can all be halved or doubled easily. Just remember that ¼ cup = 4 tablespoons.

For those with special dietary considerations, many recipes are vegetarian
or can be easily made to be vegetarian. The dairy (milk powder and cheese) in
some of the recipes is optional, including in the cereals. My dairy-free friend
Tracey commented after she field-tested many of them: "For those of us who
don't eat it, dairy isn't missed at all."

All the pack-and-go trail recipes list the ingredients according to how you
will package them. Freezer-weight self-sealing bags in varying sizes work best
for transport. A two-quart bag will hold all the ingredients (which may be in
several labeled bags inside the large one) for up to eight servings. On the
outer bag, be sure to write the instructions for putting the recipe together. It's

Adding Water While Cooking

Adding water to these recipes requires more thoughtfulness than methodology. You must use your judgment when adding the water to the recipes; depending on the efficiency of your stove, the dryness of the ingredients, and the weather, you may need more or less. If your stove simmers hot, if the humidity in the air is low (dry), or if the ingredients are commercially dried, you may need more water. It is possible, but not likely, that you will need less under other circumstances.

The water for the recipe can be boiled first for purposes of purification. Always start with less water than is listed in the recipe and add more as needed. When a recipe calls for a sauce, it should be thick. Only the soups are meant to be soupy. Pasta need not be drained unless the recipe calls for it.

also a good idea to copy the instructions onto a card and keep it with the food so there is no confusion about how it all goes together. The packages or pouches are listed in the recipe in the order in which they are used.

The instructions for each package differ:

- **All-in-one pouch:** These ingredients require no rehydration or cooking; just add water.

- **Rehydration pouch:** These ingredients should be rehydrated in advance and go into the pot first to simmer and finish rehydrating.

- **Add-and-cook pouch:** These ingredients are added when the ingredients in the rehydration pouch have rehydrated and/or when the water has come to a boil.

- **Final-additions pouch:** These ingredients do not need to cook for long; they are added to the hot recipe at the end of cooking and mixed in.

- **Mix-and-make pouch:** These ingredients require separate mixing and then need to cook either separately (bannock) or toward the end of the cooking process (dumplings).

- **Finishing-touches pouch:** These items go on top as a garnish after serving the food.

- **Preparation tips:** This is information specific to the recipe or ingredients.

Dehydrating How-To

Fruits and Vegetables

✔ Mince, shred, or chop before you dehydrate. Prepare the foods the way you want them to come out in the final recipe.

✔ Always blanch vegetables that you want to be soft in the recipe, such as carrots, peas, corn, and cabbage. Softer vegetables like tomatoes, mushrooms, peppers, and onions do not require blanching. The best way to blanch the cut-up or shredded vegetables is to put them in a sieve or steamer basket and immerse them either in boiling water or steam (my preferred method), stirring once until the color darkens slightly. This takes only a minute or two, so watch careful-ly. Run the vegetables immediately under cold water to prevent further cooking. Blanching can also be done in a microwave, but this is harder to control, so I don't recommend it. Be fussy about your blanching so you don't end up cooking your vegetables—they'll turn to mash in the final recipe.

✔ Frozen vegetables are a great timesaver because they are already prepared, chopped, and blanched. Don't even bother thawing them; just put them in the dehydrator.

✔ Dehydrate fruits and vegetables at a low temperature (120 to 130 degrees Fahrenheit) so that they retain flavor and color. The end result should be pliable, not brittle.

✔ Do not dehydrate strongly flavored foods together with mild flavors; otherwise, the milder fla-vors will be lost or tainted. It's best to dry fruits with fruits, vegetables with vegetables, meat with meat, and nothing else with onions or soap.

Leathers

✔ For leathers, spread ingredients ¼-inch thick on waxed paper or parchment paper sprayed with cooking oil spray. When finished and cooled, peel off the paper and tear the leather into strips.

✔ Leathers should dehydrate slowly at a low temperature (110 to 120 degrees Fahrenheit). Watch; you don't want it to get so dry that cracks form.

Meats

✔ Meats and seafood should be fully cooked and dried at high temperatures (135 to 145 degrees Fahrenheit) to prevent bacterial growth.

✔ Before putting meat in the dehydrator, rinse off as much fat as possible to prevent rancidity. An easy way to do this is to put the cooked meat in a strainer. Place this in a lower, wider bowl and run water through the meat so that the water overflows the bowl. When the water runs clear, the meat is rinsed.

Dehydrating Your Food

Food dehydration is one the easiest and most rewarding tasks that accompa-nies camp food preparation, if you have a decent dehydrator. Fresh local pro-duce retains much of its flavor if it's dehydrated soon after being picked, and unusual and interesting ingredients can be introduced into your recipes. Home-drying is also a thrifty way to produce camp food. If you dry most of

How Dry Is It?

Drying times will vary according to humidity, size of the food pieces, altitude, ripeness, and other factors. Food will reduce in volume by about half or less. It should be consistently darkened in color and show no evidence of moisture inside or out. Until you're used to dehydrating food, you can check to ensure that you have fully cured the food by placing it for a day in a closed glass jar, in the light of a window. If any moisture forms on the jar, you need to return the food to the dehydrator.

your ingredients, you can feed a group with large-size gourmet meals, snacks, and extras for less than $12 a day per person. Nothing need ever go bad in your fridge again. When you're not dehydrating food for camping, the dehydrator does wonderful things with flowers and herbs.

Oven-Drying

Drying can be done in an oven, but this is more work-intensive and the results are not as predictable. The heat is difficult to regulate and must be monitored with an oven thermometer. It's not very energy-efficient, either, since the drying times are longer and the oven's heating element will run almost continuously. A dehydrator pays for itself soon enough in energy savings.

If you really want to use your oven, you will also need to make drying racks. Most regular ovens can accommodate four racks. Lightweight pegboard or vinyl window screening stapled to a 1-by-1-inch frame works well. Do not use any metal (other than screws or staples) in making racks. Make the racks at least 6 inches shorter than the front-to-back width of the oven so they can be staggered for better airflow.

Instant Instant Oatmeal

Make your own instant oatmeal by grinding two-thirds of a bag of quick oats in the blender until it is mealy. Mix it back in with the unground oats–*et voilà!*

When using an oven, wedge the door open 1 inch with a wooden spoon for the duration of the drying time. Do not put any rack closer than 6 inches from the heating element—farther if it's vinyl screening. Because the heat and air do not circulate evenly, rearrange the food often to ensure consistent drying.

Luckily, many people have bought dehydrators and never figured out what to do with them, so they tend to be garage-sale items. If you're still considering using the oven, you probably also do all the work-intensive Martha Stewart stuff. Don't say I didn't tell you. Buy or borrow a dehydrator. It's way easier.

Dehydrator Rack Covers

Using sheer nylon of the type used for sheer curtains, make screens for your dehydrator racks. The lighter the fabric, the better, as you do not want to inhibit airflow—but don't use cheesecloth, because the food sticks to it. Cut the fabric to fit your trays. The fabric screens keep food from falling through the racks, make it easier to empty the trays, and are easier to wash than racks with food dried on them.

Handling Dehydrated Food

Store dried foods individually in airtight freezer bags in the freezer. This ensures the freshness of the foods until it's time to assemble the recipe. If your freezer isn't frost-free, double-bag so that moisture doesn't get into the food. Then put it in the dehydrator for an hour when it comes out of the freezer.

In the week before your trip, assemble the recipes in freezer-weight, self-sealing bags that can be labeled with the directions. Smaller bags can be used for some ingredients, and all the bags can usually go in one large-sized bag with the starch for the meal. Write the preparation directions on the outer bag with a waterproof marker.

Storing and assembling the individual ingredients maintains the integrity of the recipes. If you assemble the recipe and then dry it, or if you store the recipe assembled, then you will have the equivalent of what can be bought at the store—a plate of food with a single flavor and consistency. Even though you are eating primarily one-dish meals, there's no reason to eat gruel. It doesn't take any more time to prepare the ingredients separately, but the difference in flavors and textures is rewarding. It's possible to eat very well and not compromise the standards of lightweight, low-impact camping. Other than flatbreads, you can avoid taking any perishable foods whatsoever. And if you're hungry and enjoying fresh air, friends, and a beautiful vista, the meals will be superb.

I have found some items inexpensive enough to purchase, while home-drying them may be work-intensive or produce unreliable results. Also, freeze-dried starches shorten the cooking time. I don't bother home-drying when I can't improve on the finished product. Still, don't let *my* shortcomings limit your imagination. Anything can be dried with good results. I find that if the key flavors in a recipe are home-dried, then it doesn't matter if the starch or some of the lesser ingredients aren't. Some items that I usually buy in bulk already dry include:

- ✔ Fruits such as currants, raisins, cranberries, and sometimes apples, apricots, peaches, and pears. Seasonal berries and kiwi are excellent when home-dried and will really add to your mixed-fruit concoctions.

- ✔ Pastas, instant rice, mashed potatoes, and polenta.

- ✔ Sun-dried tomatoes.

- ✔ Falafel and refried beans.

- ✔ Onion flakes—only because my family will not let me dry cooking onions in the house. They draw the line at leeks and scallions, which still do a fairly potent job of ensuring that everyone's tear ducts are clear.

Basic Recipes for Dehydrating Ingredients at Home

Ground Meat

Extra-lean hamburger, ground pork, or other ground meat
(¼ lb. for every 2 people eating the final recipe)
Garlic powder, salt, and pepper to taste

Sauté the meat with the seasoning, breaking it into small pieces and cooking it until all the red is gone. Rinse the meat in a colander until the water runs clear of fat. Spread the meat onto a tray and dehydrate for 6 to 8 hours in your oven at 200° F, in a dehydrator at 145° F, or according to the manufacturer's directions.

Pam's Always-Tender Chicken

Chicken thighs (1 large thigh for every 2 people eating the final recipe if it's a soup or stew)

For every four thighs, add:
½ cup diced onion and celery
1 tsp. poultry seasoning
salt and pepper to taste

Cover the chicken thighs and onion and celery with seasoned water. Boil until the chicken is cooked through, and then drain the stock. You may reserve the broth for future use as chicken stock. Remove all skin, fat, and bones from the chicken, rinse, and cut into chunks. Spread the meat on a tray and dehydrate for 6 to 8 hours in your oven at 200° F, in a dehydrator at 145° F, or according to manufacturer's directions.

Jamie's Beef Jerky

Any lean roast or thick cut of beef (2–3 lbs.)

Marinade:
½ cup soy sauce
¼ cup brown sugar
1 tsp. ground ginger
2 cloves garlic, crushed
¼ tsp. black pepper

Remove all visible fat from the roast and slice the meat, with the grain, into ¼-inch strips. Put the meat into a nonmetal container; pour the marinade over it and toss. Cover with plastic wrap and refrigerate overnight, stirring a few times. Spread the meat on a tray and dehydrate for 6 to 8 hours in your oven at 200° F, in a dehydrator at 145° F, or according to manufacturer's directions. Dry until leathery, but still bendable. Wrap it in paper towel when removing it from the dehydrator to remove any remaining fat.

Tofu Jerky

Cake of extra-firm tofu

Marinade:
½ cup soy sauce
¼ cup water
1 tbsp. Worcestershire sauce
1 tbsp. honey
1 tsp. each paprika and onion powder
2 cloves garlic, crushed
1 tsp. black pepper

Drain and slice the tofu into ¼-inch strips. Mix the marinade well. Place the tofu on a cookie sheet in a single layer and pour the marinade over it. Cover with plastic wrap and refrigerate overnight, turning once. Spread the tofu on a tray and dehydrate for 4 to 6 hours in your oven at 150° F, in a dehydrator at 125° F, or according to manufacturer's directions. Dry until leathery but still bendable.

Sweet Tofu Jerky

Cake of extra-firm tofu

Marinade:
¼ cup maple syrup
¼ cup water
2 tsp. soy sauce
2 tsp. dark brown sugar

Drain and slice the tofu into ¼-inch strips. Mix the marinade well. Place the tofu on a cookie sheet in a single layer and pour the marinade over it. Cover with plastic wrap and refrigerate overnight, turning once. Spread the tofu on to a tray and dehydrate for 4 to 6 hours in your oven at 150° F, in a dehydrator at 125° F, or according to manufacturer's directions. Dry until leathery but still bendable.

Tomato Leather

For each 10-by-10-inch (or 12-inch round dehydrator tray) sheet of
tomato leather, use:

1 5½-oz. can tomato paste
1 tsp. minced onion
¼ tsp. minced garlic
pinch each of powdered basil, oregano, and thyme
salt and pepper to taste

Place all ingredients into a nonstick pan. Simmer slowly for 15 minutes,
stirring occasionally so that all the flavors are mingled. Spread ¼ inch
thick on waxed paper or parchment paper sprayed with cooking oil spray.
Dehydrate for 8 to 10 hours in your oven at 150° F, in a dehydrator at
115° F, or according to manufacturer's directions. When finished, peel off
the paper and tear the leather into strips.

Salsa Leather

For each 10-by-10-inch (or 12-inch round dehydrator tray) sheet of salsa
leather, use:

½ 5½-oz. can tomato paste
½ cup commercial salsa, as hot as you like it
pinch each of powdered garlic and oregano
½ tsp. each grated lime zest and finely chopped cilantro

Mix all ingredients in a nonmetal bowl. Mix well, cover, and let sit in a
refrigerator overnight. Spread ¼ inch thick on waxed paper or parchment
paper sprayed with cooking oil spray. Dehydrate for 8 to 10 hours in your
oven at 150° F, in a dehydrator at 115° F, or according to manufacturer's
directions. When finished, peel off the paper and tear the leather into
strips.

Bannock and Breakfast

Making Bannock

Bannock has always been the easiest of recipes to prepare for camp, and it's not just a breakfast food. Bannock was a staple of the early settlers and became a staple for many of North America's First Nations. Basically toasting, frying, or pan-baking any good biscuit recipe will produce bannock. When virtually everything is dehydrated, bannock is an easy "fresh" addition to your menu.

All of the following recipes can be made ahead and put in a sturdy zipper-locking bag. Shortening can be used instead of lard; increasing its amount will make a more tender biscuit.

When you're ready to use the dough, just add enough water to the bag a tablespoon at a time to create a soft, sticky dough and knead it (as little as possible) in the bag. Cook it in a frying pan with the lid on, slowly over low heat or over coals.

If you can't get a low heat on your backpacking stove (a common problem), or if the pan you cook it in doesn't distribute the heat well, bring a pie tin that fits the bottom of your pan without nesting it. You can use that to disperse the heat.

Bannock Bob's Bannock

Tea-Bisk, Bisquick, or any biscuit mix
instant dried milk

Preparation tips: Follow the directions on the package for quantities and add enough water to make a stiff dough. Bake over low heat or coals in a heavy pan or patted into a thin bun on the end of a toasting stick.

Elaine's Scratch Bannock

Elaine makes the best bannock that I have ever had. She tells me it is derived from a heritage recipe in an old book called *The Laura Secord Canadian Cookbook.*

Sift and blend:
2¾ cups all-purpose flour
2 tsp. baking powder
½ tsp. salt

Cut in with two knives or a pastry blender:

3 tbsp. lard

Add:

¼ cup raisins (if desired)

On the trail, mix in:

up to ⅔ cup water

Preparation tips: Bake over low heat or coals in a lightly greased, heavy pan or patted into a thin bun on the end of a toasting stick. Makes 8 biscuits or 1 pan.

Molasses Bannock

Serve hot with maple syrup. Make enough at breakfast to have for lunch with peanut butter and jam or to serve as a dessert topped with stewed dried apples in brown sugar syrup.

Blend:

2 cups all-purpose flour

2½ tsp. baking powder

½ tsp. baking soda

1 tsp. dehydrated grated orange peel

¼ cup instant dried milk

½ tsp. cinnamon

¼ tsp. nutmeg

¼ tsp. ground ginger

¼ tsp. salt

Cut in with two knives or a pastry blender:

¼ cup butter

¼ cup molasses

Add:

¼ cup chopped pecans or walnuts (if desired)

On the trail, mix in:

up to ⅔ cup water

Preparation tips: Pat into small patties. Bake over low heat or coals in a lightly greased, heavy pan. Makes 8 biscuits.

Focaccia-Style Bannock

Serve with pasta and tomato sauce.

Blend:

2½ cups all-purpose flour

2 tsp. baking powder

½ tsp. salt

1 tsp. oregano

½ tsp. basil

½ cup Parmesan or Romano cheese

Cut in with two knives or a pastry blender:

2 tbsp. butter creamed together with 1½ tbsp. extra-virgin olive oil

On the trail, mix in:

up to ⅔ cup water

Preparation tips: Pat into small patties. Bake over low heat or coals in a lightly greased, heavy pan. Makes 8 biscuits.

Other Breakfast Items

Cereal bars, dried fruit, and cheese with a hot drink make a quick breakfast—but everyone loves a hot breakfast on the trail if you can afford the time. Any hot cereal is easy enough to take and make, but following are some tasty alternatives.

Strawberry Banana Yogurt Cereal

Add-and-cook pouch:

½ sheet banana-honey yogurt leather

¼ cup sliced strawberries or whole blueberries, dehydrated

½ cup quick cream of wheat

½ cup instant dried milk

1 tsp. sugar

Add to:

3 cups boiling water

Preparation tips: To make the yogurt leather for this recipe, blend together a banana, 1 tbsp. honey, and 8 oz. plain or berry yogurt until smooth. Spread ¼ inch thick on waxed paper or parchment paper sprayed with cooking oil spray. Dehydrate for 8 to 10 hours in your oven at 150° F, in a dehydrator at 115° F, or according to manufacturer's directions. When finished, peel off the paper and tear the leather into strips.

Milk Toast

There was a time when milk toast was dispensed to every child who was sick. It consisted of warmed sweetened milk poured over a piece of toast. Even in the following version, it tastes like comfort food.

All-in-one pouch:
2 cups Grape-Nuts cereal
½ cup instant dried milk
¼ cup brown sugar
½ tsp. cinnamon
¼ tsp. nutmeg
2 tbsp. raisins (optional)

Preparation tips: Make in the bowls by adding 1/2 cup boiling water per bowl.

No-Bake Quiche

In my quest to come up with a decent dried-egg breakfast, this evolved. It's a bit work-intensive, though.

Add-and-cook pouch:
½ cup julienne ham, dehydrated
¼ cup coarsely chopped spinach leaves, dehydrated
½ tsp. dried onion
1 packet vegetable bouillon

Add to:
1 cup boiling water

Add to the above when rehydrated and boiling:
1 packet gelatin powder

Final-additions pouch:
1 cup milk powder
4 tbsp. powdered eggs

½ cup cheddar cheese powder

¼ tsp. mustard powder

1 tbsp. parsley flakes

1 tbsp. dried chives

fresh grating of pepper

Add and mix well:

2 cups cold water

Mix-and-make pouch:

any good plain bannock recipe (see Elaine's Scratch Bannock)

Preparation tips: Make the quiche the night before so that it has time to set. Pour the hot gelatin mixture into the cold-water pouch, mix, and cache it someplace cool for the night. In the morning, pat the bannock into thin cakes and fry. Serve the cooled quiche on the hot bannock.

Bobbi's Favorite Breakfast

Fellow campers either love or hate this one, but it's my favorite.

Add-and-cook pouch:

¾ cup dried fruits, chopped

Add to:

3 cups boiling water

All-in-one pouch:

1½ cups instant oatmeal

¼ cup instant dried milk

¾ cup granola

4 tsp. brown sugar

Preparation tips: Pour the hot fruit and juice over top of the cereal in your bowl and mix.

Rice Cereal with Apricots

Add-and-cook pouch:

1½ cups instant rice

¾ cup dried apricot bits

2 tbsp. brown sugar

1 cup instant dried milk

½ tsp. cinnamon

Add to:

3 cups boiling water

Cranberry Orange Cereal

This recipe can be rehydrated the night before and served cold in the morning. Or it can be cooked in the morning with no rehydration necessary.

Rehydration pouch (to serve cold), or add-and-cook pouch (to serve hot):

1½ cups bulghur wheat

¾ cup dried cranberries

2 tbsp. brown sugar

¼ cup orange juice crystals

1 tsp. dried orange zest (grated peel)

Add:

3 cups water

Final-additions pouch:

½ cup toasted chopped walnuts

Lunch

When you can, lunchtime is a good time to take an extended break to revive and refresh yourselves. Like breakfast, lunch can consist of "pickup" foods such as jerky, cheese, peanut butter, bars, and dried fruit. Crispbreads and toasts are dense, lightweight, and so easy to pack, and together with instant noodles or instant soups make a tasty lunch. The recipes offered here are instant or need only to be rehydrated in the morning to be ready for lunch. They are flavorful and make a fast and pleasing addition to the menu.

Hummus

In your kitchen, combine:

1 19-oz. can chickpeas, drained, liquid reserved
2 cloves garlic
2 tbsp. tahini (sesame seed paste)
juice of 1 lemon
1 tsp. sugar

Place everything in a blender or food processor and blend until smooth, adding more of the reserved liquid as necessary for blending only. Spread ¼ inch thick on waxed paper or parchment paper sprayed with cooking oil spray. Dehydrate for 6 to 8 hours in your oven at 150° F, in a dehydrator at 115° F, or according to manufacturer's directions. When finished, the dehydrated hummus will crumble. Store and carry in a rehydration pouch.

On the trail:

Dehydrated hummus rehydrates instantly when you add ½ cup water.

Add to rehydration pouch:

1 tbsp. sesame seeds

To serve:

Serve as a spread in a pita or tortilla wrap with sliced fresh vegetables on day 1 or 2. Or eat on pitas with tabouli or lentil salad. Makes about 2 cups of hummus.

Four-Layer Burrito

Rehydration pouch 1:

½ 10-by-10-inch sheet salsa leather

¼ cup small chunks avocado, dehydrated

Add:

approximately ¼ cup water

Rehydration pouch 2:

½ cup TVP (textured vegetable protein, available in health food stores)

1 tsp. dried onion flakes

2 tsp. taco seasoning mix

Add:

approximately ¼ cup water

Rehydration pouch 3:

½ cup refried beans, dehydrated

Add:

approximately ¼ cup water or per package directions

Finishing-touches pouches:

1 cup shredded cheddar cheese

8 tortillas (7½-inch diameter)

Preparation tips: Layer the rehydrated ingredients (no cooking necessary) in a tortilla and roll. These can be eaten cold but are best rolled, then heated over low heat in a covered frying pan with a little oil.

Sweet Pepper Lentil Salad

This is great on spinach leaves or pitas with crackers and cheese on the side.

Rehydration pouch:

1 cup cooked or canned lentils, dehydrated (about 1 19-oz. can, drained)

¼ cup diced red pepper, dehydrated

½ sheet Ajvar (red pepper spread) leather

½ sheet plain yogurt leather

½ tsp. sugar

1 tsp. garlic powder

¼ tsp. cayenne

Add:

2 cups water

Preparation tips: Jarred European red pepper spread or Ajvar can be found in health food stores. Both the Ajvar and plain yogurt can be used as is and spread ¼ inch thick on waxed paper or parchment paper sprayed with cooking oil spray. Dehydrate for 6 to 8 hours in your oven at 150° F, in a dehydrator at 115° F, or according to manufacturer's directions. When finished, peel off the paper and tear the leather into strips. The Ajvar may crumble when dry.

Savory Cheese Spuds

All-in-one pouch:
1 cup instant potatoes
¼ cup instant dried milk
¼ cup powdered cheese sauce
1 tbsp. bacon TVP (textured vegetable protein) bits or dried bacon bits
2 tsp. parsley flakes
1 tbsp. dried chives
¼ tsp. each of mustard powder and paprika
salt and pepper

Make in the bowls:
Add ¾ cup boiling water per bowl.

Finishing touches:
Some people like ketchup on this.

Preparation tips: Follow the package directions if they differ for 4 cups of mashed potatoes.

Cashew Wraps

Rehydration pouch:
¾ cup dehydrated shredded cabbage
1 cup fine rice noodles or rice sticks, broken up
¼ cup dehydrated unsweetened canned crushed pineapple
2 tbsp. dried onion flakes
4 tbsp. flaked unsweetened coconut

2 tbsp. dehydrated grated daikon (Japanese radish)

Add:

1½ cups water

Final-additions pouch:

1 cup toasted cashew pieces

2 tbsp. soy sauce (I save the Chinese restaurant take-out pouches)

Finishing-touches pouch:

8 tortillas (7½-inch diameter)

Wrap ½ cup of filling into each tortilla.

Preparation tips: For a hot dish, rehydrate by adding to boiling water and heat the tortillas on the pot lid.

Tabouli Salad

Rehydration pouch:

¾ cup bulghur wheat

1 cup dehydrated broken tomato slices

¼ cup parsley flakes

2 tsp. dehydrated sliced black olives

¼ cup dehydrated crumbled feta cheese

3 tbsp. dehydrated chopped leeks or spring onions

1 tbsp. oregano

1 tsp. garlic powder

salt and pepper

Add:

2 cups water

Drain any excess liquid before adding the dressing.

Dressing (in leakproof plastic bottle):

3 tbsp. olive oil

2 tbsp. lemon juice

Finishing-touches pouch:

pita bread

Preparation tips: Spoon into pita pockets. Feta cheese can be rinsed and cut into ¼-inch slices to dehydrate. Crumble it after it has dehydrated.

Supper

Go all out at supper and reward yourselves with a great meal and dessert. Boxed wine can be "decanted" from the box; it travels easily in the bag, and the vintages in boxes are improving. If you choose to bring wine to accompany your meals, imbibe moderately. You need to be alert to your surroundings and be able to respond effectively to risks in the backcountry.

Spanish Rice

Rehydration pouch:
½ cup dehydrated hamburger

1 sheet tomato leather

¼ cup dehydrated corn

¼ cup dehydrated chopped green peppers

2 tbsp. dehydrated chopped onions

2 tbsp. dehydrated sliced mushrooms

Add:
1 cup water

Add-and-cook pouch:
1½ cups instant rice

4 tsp. taco seasoning (1 package)

Add:
approximately 2 more cups water

Finishing-touches pouch:
½ cup grated cheddar cheese

Preparation tips: If substituting TVP (textured vegetable protein) for the hamburger, put it in with the rice.

Alfredo Rice Divan

Rehydration pouch:
¼ cup dehydrated julienne ham

¼ cup dehydrated sliced mushrooms

¼ cup dehydrated cut-up broccoli or asparagus

Add:

1 cup water

Add-and-cook pouch 1:

1½ cups instant rice

Add:

2 cups water

Add-and-cook pouch 2:

1 package Alfredo sauce mix
¼ cup instant dried milk
¼ cup grated Romano cheese
1 tsp. parsley flakes
½ tsp. dried chives

Add:

water as necessary to make a thick sauce

Preparation tips: A splash of white wine is nice in this if you have it.

Shrimp and Wild Rice Pilaf

Rehydration pouch:

½ cup dehydrated cooked shrimp
½ cup dehydrated frozen peas-and-carrots mix
¼ cup dehydrated sliced mushrooms
2 tbsp. dehydrated chopped leeks
2 tbsp. dehydrated chopped red pepper

Add:

2 cups water

Add-and-cook pouch:

1 cup instant rice
½ tsp. curry powder
¼ tsp. thyme
2 tsp. parsley flakes
½ tsp. garlic powder
½ cup dehydrated or instant wild rice
1 packet powdered chicken bouillon

Add:

approximately 1 more cup water

Finishing-touches pouch:

2 tbsp. slivered almonds

1 tbsp. currants

Preparation tips: Canned or frozen cooked shrimp dehydrates well, but you'll want to give it at least 2 hours to rehydrate.

Greek Spinach Pilaf

Rehydration pouch:

1 bunch (6 oz.) fresh spinach leaves, dehydrated

½ cup dehydrated Roma tomato slices

1 tbsp. dehydrated sliced black olives

2 tbsp. dehydrated diced onion

Add:

1 cup water

Add-and-cook pouch:

2 cups instant rice

2 tsp. powdered vegetable broth

¼ cup dehydrated feta cheese, crumbled

1 tsp. thyme

2 tsp. mint

2 tsp. oregano

freshly ground pepper

Add:

approximately 2 cups water

Finishing-touches pouch:

2 tbsp. chopped dates

Preparation tips: To dehydrate feta cheese, rinse it and cut into ¼-inch slices. Crumble it after it has dehydrated.

Middle Eastern Lentils and Couscous

Rehydration pouch:

¼ cup dehydrated sliced carrots

¼ cup dehydrated grated cabbage

¼ cup dehydrated cubed potatoes

2 tbsp. dehydrated chopped red bell peppers

1 tsp. curry powder

1 tsp. ground coriander

2 tsp. ground cumin

¼ tsp. red pepper flakes (to taste)

Add:

1 cup water

Add-and-cook pouch 1:

1 19-oz. can lentils, dehydrated, or 1 cup red lentils (red lentils will cook in
   20 minutes)

2 tbsp. powdered vegetable broth

Add:

approximately 1 cup water

Add-and-cook pouch 2:

1 cup couscous (will cook in 5–10 minutes)

Add:

approximately 1 cup water

Preparation tips: If you're using red lentils, bring them to a boil first and
then add the rehydrating vegetables so that the lentils soften. When
everything is soft, add the couscous and enough water to finish cooking.

Imperial Couscous

Rehydration pouch:

¼ cup dehydrated coarsely grated turnip

¼ cup dehydrated coarsely grated carrots

¼ cup dehydrated coarsely grated yam

¼ cup dehydrated sliced leeks

2 tbsp. dehydrated thinly sliced orange or red pepper

3 tbsp. chili powder

1 tbsp. garlic powder

1 tsp. brown sugar

freshly grated pepper

Add:

1 cup water

Add-and-cook pouch:

1 cup couscous

¼ cup dried cranberries

1 packet powdered chicken bouillon

¼ cup currants

Add:

approximately 2 cups water

Finishing touches pouch:

3 tbsp. toasted sliced almonds

Black Bean Chili

Rehydration pouch:

1 cup dehydrated cooked or canned black beans

2 tbsp. dehydrated diced carrots

2 tbsp. dehydrated corn

2 tbsp. dehydrated diced green pepper

1 tbsp. French onion soup mix

Add:

2 cups water

Add-and-cook pouch:

1 tsp. dehydrated sliced jalapeño

½ sheet tomato leather

¼ cup currants

2 tbsp. TVP (textured vegetable protein)

1 tbsp. chili powder

½ tsp. ground cumin

½ tsp. garlic powder

Add:

approximately 1 cup water

Finishing-touches pouch:

½ cup crushed tortilla chips

Chicken Stew with Dumplings

Rehydration pouch:

½ cup dehydrated chicken chunks (see Pam's Always-Tender Chicken)

1 cup dehydrated frozen mixed vegetables

¼ cup dehydrated sliced mushrooms

1 tsp. dehydrated onion flakes

¼ sheet tomato leather

2 tbsp. mushroom soup mix

1 tsp. poultry seasoning

½ tsp. garlic powder

½ tsp. oregano

freshly ground pepper, to taste

Add:

approximately 2 cups water

Add-and-cook pouch:

2 tbsp. instant potatoes

Add:

approximately 1 cup water

Dumplings (mix-and-make pouch):

1 cup biscuit mix

2 tbsp. instant dried milk

Preparation tips: Add instant potatoes and more water if necessary to create a thin sauce. Add enough water to the dumpling mix to make a stiff dough in the bag. Knead well and cut off the bottom corner to squeeze out golf-ball-sized pieces directly into the stew. Cover and simmer for at least 10 minutes over very low heat. The dumplings should be dry inside when ready to eat.

Wild Mushroom and Jerky Stew

Rehydration pouch 1:

4–5 strips beef jerky, cut or broken into small pieces

2 tbsp. French onion soup mix

1 tsp. oregano

Add:

1 cup water

Rehydration pouch 2:

¼ cup dehydrated oyster and portobello mushrooms, cut in strips

2 tbsp. dehydrated sliced regular mushrooms

½ cup dehydrated potato slices

2 tbsp. dehydrated sliced leeks

2 tbsp. mushroom soup mix

½ tsp. garlic powder

½ tsp. paprika

Add:

1½ cups water

Add-and-cook pouch:

red wine

Mix the rehydrated ingredients together and cook until soft with a little red wine if you have it.

Finishing-touches pouch

Use instant potatoes to thicken the gravy.

Preparation tips: Serve with bannock or use half of the Focaccia-Style Bannock recipe to make dumplings.

Shepherd's Pie

Rehydration pouch:

1 cup dehydrated hamburger

1 cup dehydrated peas and corn

2 tbsp. dehydrated chopped mushrooms

1 tsp. dried onion flakes

1 packet powdered beef bouillon

freshly grated pepper

Add:

2 cups water

Add-and-cook pouch:

1 package brown gravy mix

Add:

approximately 1 cup water

Final-additions pouch:

½ cup instant mashed potatoes
2 tbsp. instant dried milk
2 tsp. Parmesan cheese
1 tsp. garlic powder
1 tsp. parsley flakes

Preparation tips: Add the gravy bag when the meat and vegetables are ready for serving. Divide the final additions into 4 bowls and add approximately ½ cup boiling water to each bowl. Mix the garlic mashed potatoes in your bowl and serve the stew on top. Follow the package directions if they differ for 2 cups of mashed potatoes.

Cheesy Vegetable Soup

Rehydration pouch:

1 cup dried soup vegetables
¼ cup dehydrated cooked or canned pinto or navy beans
¼ cup powdered vegetable broth

Add:

2 cups water

Add-and-cook pouch:

½ cup powdered cheddar cheese
¼ cup instant dried milk

Add:

approximately 2 cups water

Finishing-touches pouch:

crostini bread or croutons
½ cup sunflower seeds

Preparation tips: Pour the soup over the bread and top with sunflower seeds. If you're using purchased soup vegetables, allow extra rehydration time.

Corn Chowder

Rehydration pouch:

½ cup dehydrated corn

½ cup dehydrated cubed potatoes

2 tbsp. dried onion

¼ cup powdered vegetable broth

Add:

2 cups water

Add-and-cook pouch:

½ cup instant dried milk

¼ cup instant mashed potatoes

1 tsp. parsley flakes

½ tsp. marjoram or chervil

1 tsp. sugar

freshly grated pepper

Add:

approximately 2 cups water

Preparation tips: Serve this with Molasses Bannock.

Beef and Barley Soup

Rehydration pouch 1:

¼ cup dehydrated diced carrots

2 tbsp. dehydrated diced celery

2 tbsp. dehydrated diced zucchini

2 tbsp. dehydrated diced spring onions

¼ cup dehydrated cooked barley

¼ cup dehydrated canned or cooked lentils

1 packet powdered vegetable bouillon

1 bay leaf

Add:

1½ cups water

Rehydration pouch 2:

½ cup dehydrated hamburger

½ sheet tomato leather

2 tbsp. French onion soup mix

1 packet powdered beef bouillon

1 tsp. garlic powder

Add:

1½ cups water

Add-and-cook pouch:

1 tsp. parsley flakes

½ tsp. thyme

½ tsp. basil

Add: *2 cups water*

Preparation tips: At home, cook ¼ cup barley in 1½ cups water flavored with Worcestershire sauce. When soft, drain and dehydrate.

West Coast Asian Casserole

Rehydration pouch:

½ cup dehydrated cubed chicken or ground pork

½ cup dehydrated bean sprouts

20 dehydrated snow peas

20 dehydrated spinach leaves

¼ cup dehydrated sliced zucchini

¼ cup dehydrated sliced daikon (Japanese radish)

¼ cup dehydrated sliced green pepper

1 tsp. dried onion flakes

Add:

2 cups water

Add-and-cook pouch:

2 3–4 oz. packages instant noodles

1 packet chicken bouillon powder

½ tsp. ground ginger

1 tsp. garlic powder

freshly grated pepper

Add:

approximately 1 cup water

Add-and-cook 2 (in leakproof plastic bottle):

2 tbsp. brown sugar

2 tbsp. soy sauce

2 tsp. white vinegar

2 tbsp. cornstarch

Finishing-touches pouch:

2 tbsp. sesame seeds

Tuna Parmesan Casserole

Rehydration pouch:

¼ cup dehydrated tuna

¼ cup dehydrated peas

2 tbsp. dehydrated chopped green pepper

2 tbsp. dehydrated sliced red pepper

1 tbsp. dried onion flakes

2 tbsp. French onion soup mix

Add:

1 cup water

Add-and-cook pouch:

2 cups egg noodles

½ tsp. thyme

fresh grating of pepper

½ tsp. paprika

½ tsp. garlic powder

Add:

approximately 2 cups water (only enough for the pasta to cook without draining)

Final-additions pouch:

¼ cup Parmesan cheese

¼ cup instant dried milk

Kitsilano Rice and Bean Casserole

Rehydration pouch:

1 cup dehydrated cooked turtle (black) beans

¼ cup dehydrated diced green pepper

¼ cup dried onion flakes

2 tbsp. dehydrated sliced green olives

½ sheet tomato leather

Add:

2 cups water

Add-and-cook pouch:

1 tsp. garlic powder

½ tsp. thyme

½ tsp. basil

½ tsp. oregano

½ cup instant brown rice

1 tsp. TVP (textured vegetable protein) bacon bits

2 tbsp. mushroom soup mix

Add:

approximately 1 cup water

Sun-Dried Tomato and White Bean Polenta

Rehydration pouch:

½ cup dehydrated cooked or canned white kidney beans

½ cup sun-dried tomatoes, chopped

2 tbsp. dehydrated chopped leeks

Add:

approximately 2 cups water

Bring to a boil when rehydrated.

Add-and-cook pouch:

1 packet powdered vegetable bouillon

½ tsp. garlic powder

½ tsp. basil

½ tsp. thyme

freshly grated pepper

Mix-and-make pouch (in a separate pot):

1 cup instant polenta

Add to:

1 cup boiling water

Preparation tips: Serve the sauce over the polenta. If you can't find instant polenta, then at home make 2 cups with fine cornmeal, salt, and pepper, and spread it ¼ inch thick on the tray to dehydrate. It will crumble when dry.

Ratatouille with Orzo Casserole

Rehydration pouch:

½ cup dehydrated roasted cubed eggplant
¼ cup dehydrated sliced zucchini
¼ cup sun-dried tomatoes
¼ cup dehydrated chopped green pepper
2 tbsp. dehydrated sliced mushrooms
½ sheet tomato leather

Add:

2 cups water

Add-and-cook pouch:

¾ cup orzo
½ tsp. garlic powder
½ tsp. oregano
½ tsp. thyme
½ tsp. marjoram
¼ tsp. rosemary

Add:

approximately 1 cup water

Preparation tips: At home, roast a medium-sized eggplant. Cut it in ½-inch cubes and place in a plastic bag. Salt with approximately 1 tsp. salt and toss. Add 1 tbsp. olive oil to the bag and toss again. Spread it out on a baking sheet and broil until partly browned, turning once. When cool, pat with paper towel and dehydrate.

Spinach Pasta with Sun-Dried Tomato Sauce

Rehydration pouch:

6 slices dehydrated julienne ham

1 sheet tomato leather

¼ cup sun-dried tomatoes

¼ cup instant dried milk

½ tsp. basil

½ tsp. oregano

Add-and-cook pouch:

2 cups spinach pasta

Cook the pasta first, then add the rehydrated pouch.

Finishing-touches pouch:

¼ cup Parmesan cheese

¼ cup toasted pine nuts

Preparation tips: Boil the pasta in a minimum amount of water until not quite soft, then add the sauce and simmer until it's thick.

Pizza Pasta

Rehydration pouch:

1 sheet tomato leather

¼ cup dehydrated sliced mushrooms

¼ cup dehydrated cooked Italian sausage

¼ cup dehydrated chopped green pepper

¼ cup dehydrated sliced Roma tomatoes

2 tbsp. dehydrated sliced olives

Add:

1 cup water

Add-and-cook pouch:

1 cup elbow macaroni

Add:

approximately 2 cups water

Final-additions pouch:

½ cup sliced pepperoni

Finishing-touches pouch:

½ cup shredded mozzarella

¼ cup Parmesan cheese

Preparation tips: Dehydrate the Italian sausage by removing it from the casings and dehydrating like any other ground meat. Use a hard pepperoni stick and slice it for the meal so that there is no need to dehydrate it.

Pasta Fagioli

Rehydration pouch:

1 14-oz. can beans in tomato sauce (½ cup dehydrated; rinse before drying)

½ sheet tomato leather

2 tbsp. dehydrated sliced mushrooms

1 tsp. powdered rosemary

1 tsp garlic powder

Add:

1 cup water

Add-and-cook pouch:

1 cup tomato or tricolor pasta

Add:

approximately 2 cups water

Final additions pouch:

2 tbsp. mushroom soup mix

2 tbsp. instant dried milk

¼ tsp. cayenne

freshly grated pepper

Finishing-touches pouch:

¼ cup Parmesan cheese

Tofu Pesto with Three-Pepper Pasta

Rehydration pouch:

1 sheet dehydrated tofu pesto (see "Preparation tips")

2 tbsp. dehydrated julienne green pepper

2 tbsp. dehydrated julienne red pepper

2 tbsp. dehydrated julienne yellow pepper

Add-and-cook pouch:

1½ cups pasta

Cook the pasta first, then add the rehydrated pouch.

Finishing-touches pouch:

1 tbsp. olive oil in leakproof container (to sprinkle over top)
2 tbsp. grated cheese

Preparation tips: To make tofu pesto, in a blender combine 1 cup fresh basil leaves, ½ cup firm tofu, ¼ cup Romano cheese, 2 tbsp. pine nuts, 2 cloves garlic, 1 tbsp. olive oil, and ¼ tsp. salt. Blend until smooth, and spread ¼ inch thick on waxed paper to dehydrate.

Desserts

Finally, desserts are a grand reward at the end of a grand day. If you've been burning calories all day, treat yourself to one of the following delights. "Life is short, eat dessert first."

Rich Rice Pudding

Add-and-cook pouch:

1 cup instant rice

¼ cup dried currants

½ cup instant dried milk

1 tbsp. sugar

¼ tsp. nutmeg

Add to:

3 cups boiling water

Final-additions pouch:

1 package instant vanilla pudding

¼ cup white chocolate chips

Preparation tips: Allow to cool and thicken.

S'mores for the Trail

Boil-in-the-bag pouch:

½ cup milk chocolate chips

½ cup dark chocolate chips

1 cup mini marshmallows

Finishing-touches pouch:

16 graham crackers

Preparation tips: Mix the chips and marshmallows well in a freezer-weight bag. Dangle the bag in hot water until everything melts. Cut the bottom corner of the bag and squeeze onto the graham crackers.

Apple Cobbler

Add-and-cook pouch:

1½ cups dried apple rings, halved

1 packet instant cider

Add:

2 cups water

Mix-and-make pouch:

1½ cups biscuit mix

¼ cup instant dried milk

¼ cup brown sugar

½ tsp. cinnamon

¼ tsp allspice

2 tbsp. margarine

Add:

1–2 tablespoons water

Preparation tips: Add enough water to the dry ingredients to make a stiff dough and knead. When the fruit is bubbling, squeeze the dough evenly over it and push it down into the fruit a little bit. Cover and cook for about 8 more minutes until the topping is dry inside.

Tropical Fruit Pudding

Add-and-cook pouch 1:

1 cup chopped dried mango, pineapple, and/or papaya

1 tbsp. sugared ginger, chopped

½ tsp. dehydrated grated lime zest

¼ tsp. nutmeg

Add:

3 cups water

Add-and-cook pouch 2:

3 tbsp. quick-cooking tapioca

½ cup instant dried milk

Finishing-touches pouch:

½ cup crumbled banana chips

Preparation tips: At camp, simmer the fruit and gradually blend in the tapioca and milk, stirring to dissolve. Allow the pudding to cool before eating—if you can.

Berry Peach Crunch

Add-and-cook pouch 1:
½ cup dried berries
½ cup dried peach slices, chopped
¼ tsp. cinnamon
1 tsp. sugar

Add:
2 cups water

Add-and-cook pouch 2:
2 tbsp. whole wheat flour
2 tbsp. brown sugar
2 tbsp. quick oats
¼ cup chopped walnuts
¼ tsp. cinnamon
dash of cloves
1 tbsp. margarine

Add:
1 tbsp. water

Preparation tips: At camp, add water to the dry ingredients and knead. When the fruit is bubbling, sprinkle the crumble evenly over it and cook for about 6 more minutes.

Other Make-at-Home Treats

Northwest Vegetarian Pemmican

1 cup sweet tofu jerky

1 cup dried salmonberries or blueberries

1 cup unroasted sunflower seeds

2 tsp. honey

¼ cup peanut butter

½ tsp. cayenne (optional)

Preparation tips: Grind (or pound) the tofu to a mealy powder. Add the dried berries and seeds or nuts. Heat the honey, peanut butter, and cayenne until softened. Blend. Pat onto a cookie sheet. When it's cooled, slice into thin bars.

Liz's Chunky Gorp Candy

Melt together:

2 tbsp. margarine

1 9–12 oz. package unsweetened chocolate chips

1 9–12 oz. package marshmallows

½ cup peanut butter

Stir in:

½ cup each Rice Krispies, peanuts, and raisins

Preparation tips: Spread onto a nonstick or greased 9-by-13-inch pan and pat down. Refrigerate overnight and break into bite-size pieces.

Jean's Fruit Bars

Mix together:

4 cups quick-cooking oats

1 cup packed brown sugar

1 cup flaked coconut

1 cup dried chopped apricots

1 cup dried chopped cranberries

½ cup semisweet chocolate chips

Melt and whisk together:

¾ cup margarine

¾ cup orange marmalade

Preparation tips: Mix together the dry and wet ingredients. Grease a 9-by-13-inch pan, and press the mixture into it. Bake at 400°F for 20 minutes. Cool and cut into bars.

Hot Drink Recipes

When the water is boiling, take a minute to have a hot drink. Hot drinks are great when it's cold or in the evening before bed. Hot drinks can also warm and comfort the most anxious of souls.

Making a hot drink works just like the old adage that exhorted husbands to boil water when their wives were in labor. If you are in bad weather or there has been a setback or upset, boil water and make hot drinks. Friendship tea is good and quick, and the ginger coconut milk will soothe. Hot mocha will reenergize; spruce tea can keep people busy for a long time. At the first sign of disheartened folks, put the kettle on. You'll be amazed at its effectiveness.

Friendship Tea

2 cups or 2 packages iced tea mix

1 cup or 1 package lemonade crystals

1 cup or 1 package grapefruit or orange crystals

½ tsp. cinnamon

¼ tsp. cloves

Preparation tips: Blend all the ingredients. To make a cup of tea, mix 2 teaspoons in a cup of hot water. This recipe makes a lot because it's everyone's favorite. It's good hot or cold, and after dinner it tastes wonderful with a shot of cognac.

Hot Ginger Coconut Milk

2 cups instant dried milk

½ cup coconut cream powder or powdered coconut

3 tbsp. sugar

2 tbsp. ground ginger

Preparation tips: Blend all ingredients. For 1 serving, mix 3 tablespoons into a cup of hot water.

Hot Mocha

2 cups instant hot chocolate mix
1 cup instant dried milk
¼ cup sugar
¼ cup instant coffee

Preparation tips: Blend all ingredients. For 1 serving, mix 3 tablespoons into a cup of hot water

Spruce Tea

1 tsp. broken spruce needles (collected)
1 tsp. violets or strawberry flowers, crushed (collected)
4 leaves mint, crushed (collected)

Preparation tips: Add all the ingredients to 4 cups of boiling water, and steep until everything falls to the bottom. Serve with honey.

Appendix 2: Games

Following are some games that feature a good balance of skill, luck, and fun and work well on a camping trip.

Terms to Know

- Deal: Passing out the right number of cards in order (clockwise, if you're anal).

- Hand: One deal of the cards.

- Trick: One play of the cards.

- Lead: The first card played in a trick.

- Trump: The suit that carries the most weight (as in *Donald,* too).

Baffle Bridge

Players: This is a game for any number of players. If you have more than eight, then you may want to play with two decks of cards.

The deal: For the first hand, deal all the cards until everyone has the same number of cards. Put any extra cards aside to be shuffled into the next hand's deal. On the second hand, deal one less card to each person. On each successive hand, reduce the number of cards that each player has by one until everyone is playing a hand with one card dealt. Then start dealing an additional card for each hand until you're back up to the starting number of cards. The game is over when each player has the same number of cards she started with in the first hand or when everyone quits.

Trump: Each hand is played with a different trump suit. Start with clubs, then diamonds, hearts, spades, and finally no trump. Return to clubs again after a no-trump hand.

Bidding: The person to the left of the dealer decides how many tricks she will be able to take in the hand. She may claim any number of tricks based on her high cards, trump, and the number of cards dealt. It's a real guess. Each player in turn clockwise does the same. The dealer cannot bid a number that will equal the total number of tricks in the hand. For instance, if everyone has five cards and others have bid two, two, and one, then the dealer cannot bid zero. She must bid something.

The play: The person to the left of the dealer leads any card. Everyone must follow suit, and the highest card takes the trick. If a player cannot follow suit, then she may trump in. The highest trump on any trick will take it no matter what was led. Trump cannot be led until someone has played it on a trick.

Scoring: It's easiest to set up a scoring grid with the trump for each hand in a column down the left and names in a row across the top. At the start of each hand, write the bid, including no bid (zero), under each name. At the end of the hand, put a one in front of each bid that was accomplished so that zero becomes ten, one becomes eleven, etc. If the bid failed, then the number is crossed out and there is no score. Total the scores after the one-trick hand and again at the end.

Durock
Russian for "crazy," this is a favorite game in British Columbia's Doukhobor community.

Players: This is a game for any number of players. If you have more than eight, then you may want to play with two decks of cards.

The deal: Deal seven cards to each player. Place the remaining deck in the center and turn the top card over, next to the pile.

Trump: Trump is the suit of the card that is turned over next to the pile, in the deal.

The play: The person to the right of the dealer picks up the trump card and discards. She places any card from her hand faceup in front of the person to her right. If the presenter or any other player has a card with the same number as the one that has been played, she may also present it to the person who is receiving cards in this trick. The person who has received the card(s) must now "beat" the card(s) in front of her with a higher card(s) of the same suit or with a trump of any denomination. If she cannot, she must pick the card(s) up. If she lays down a card to beat the card(s) presented, and any player has a card with the same number, that player may present it to the person who is receiving cards within one minute. Only six cards in total may be presented to a receiver on any trick.

The trick ends when the receiver either beats every card that is presented or picks up all the cards presented. If the receiver beats the cards, they are removed from play and she immediately fills her hand up to seven from the center pile. She then presents to the person on her right. If the receiver is forced to pick up the cards, she misses her turn and may not present in this round of tricks.

Scoring: The play continues until the center pile is gone and players run out of cards. The winner is the first to run out of cards. The loser is the last player holding cards and is "durock" or crazy.

Hearts

This is a great game for a smaller group. Because it's loser-oriented as opposed to winner-oriented, people tend to take themselves less seriously when they play. Most people know it because it's a standard on their computer games menu.

Players: This game is best for three to five players. For three players, remove the two of clubs from the deck; for five players, remove the two and three of clubs.

The deal: Deal all the cards. Players must look at their cards and pass three cards to another player. On the first hand they pass right, on the second hand they pass left, on the third hand they pass across (if there are only three players, this one is skipped), and on the fourth hand they hold the cards, not passing.

The play: The person with the lowest club in play (either the two, three, or four) leads it. In every trick, everyone must follow suit, and the highest card of the suit that was led always takes the trick. If a player cannot follow suit, then she may play any card she likes. If a heart is "dumped" on the trick, it counts as one point against the person who takes the trick. If the queen of spades is dumped, it counts thirteen points against the person who takes the trick. Hearts cannot be led until someone has dumped it on a trick, and neither hearts nor the queen can be dumped on the first (clubs) trick. You cannot gain points in hearts, only lose them, so taking tricks is avoided particularly as play goes on.

Scoring: A total of twenty-six points are given out each hand, all of them bad. The only way to get ahead in this game is to take all the hearts and the queen of spades; called "shooting the moon," it means that everyone else gets twenty-six points against her. When a player is in the hole by one hundred points, the game ends.

Dingbat Poker

This one is wildly fun in a little two-person backpacker's tent in the rain.

Players: This game is best for two players, but more players can be introduced if they are silly enough.

The deal: Each player is given fifteen pebbles, ten matches and five Band-Aids (other items may be substituted). Two cards are dealt facedown to each player. The players simultaneously pick up the card on their right and place it facing out on their forehead without looking at it.

The play: Players may never see their own cards while the game is being played. The person who did not deal, while looking at her opponent's card, must bet. Pebbles count for one, matches for five, and Band-Aids for ten. There is a limit of five on the first round and ten on the subsequent round. The dealer bets second and must match or increase the bet, but not beyond five. After the first round of betting, each player may, in turn, choose to trade the card on her forehead for the second card by matching or increasing the bet again. If she chooses to do so, she brings it to her forehead and places the other down so she never sees what she had. If she does not want to replace the card on her forehead, she "passes." The other player in turn makes the same choice by matching the last bet. Common poker betting rules do not apply. Once both players have passed, they can put down the card they have in their hand.

Scoring: High card wins the hand and the bets.

Dingbat Poker—Archie Version

This is the one I play with my husband because he won't bluff and he won't take the second card. It's a more pragmatic game than the original.

Players: This game only works for two players.

The deal: Each player is given fifteen pebbles, ten matches, and five Band-Aids (other items may be substituted). Two cards are dealt facedown to each player. The players simultaneously pick up the card on their right and place it facing out on their forehead without looking at it.

The play: Players may never see their own cards while the game is being played. The person who did not deal, while looking at her opponent's card, must bet. Pebbles count for one, matches for five, and Band-Aids for ten. There is a limit of five on the first round and ten on the subsequent round. The dealer bets second and must match or increase the bet, but not beyond five. After the first round of betting, each player, in turn, may choose to buy the second card by matching or increasing the bet again. If she chooses to do so, she now has her pick of the better card when the play is finished. If she does not want to buy the second card, she "passes." The other player in turn makes the same choice by matching the last bet. Common poker betting rules do not apply. Once both players have passed, they can look at the cards they bought.

Scoring: High card wins the hand and the bets.

Hopscotch

One chilly, wet night, a fellow camper took a branch and scraped a hopscotch board in the dirt. An hour later, we were all warm and laughing. If you've forgotten how to play, it goes like this:

A geometric board is drawn on the ground with squares that number one to ten. The simplest way to do this is to make boxes one after the other with two boxes side by side for numbers 4 and 5 and numbers 7 and 8. The boxes should be at least 18 inches square to accommodate adult feet, but no bigger; it makes the hopping harder. There are fancier boards that you can use if someone remembers how to draw them.

Each player has a flat stone, and one begins the game by standing at the base of the board and tossing her stone into the square marked 1. That player hops on one foot (always the same foot) in squares 2 to 10, except she may put both feet down in 4 and 5, and 7 and 8. At 10 she turns on the one foot and comes back down the squares, stopping on 2 to bend over and pick up the stone as she hops off the board. A players who does this successfully, without stepping on lines or putting her other foot down, can then throw the stone into the box numbered 2 and continue to play. A player goes on until she either misses the throw into the next box, steps on a line, or falters and puts her foot down on the wrong space. The first person to finish hopping the board all the way to 10 wins.

Five Stones

This is the heritage version of the game of Jacks before some marketing guru got hold of it in the 1950s.

Five small stones or pebbles of equal size are assembled. One of the stones should have a different color or shape; this is the "jack stone." All the stones are tossed on the ground, and then the jack stone is tossed in the air. In the first round, one stone at a time is picked up during the toss. In the next round two stones are picked up in a toss, then three and four. A player's turn lasts until she makes a mistake. Variations may be introduced for skillful players, but unlike jacks, there is no bounce to prolong the time for manipulating the stones.

Appendix 3:
The Checklists

Preparedness Checkup

Not everything on this list will be applicable to what you are doing, and there may be other factors involved on your trip that are not included here and need consideration. The point of this checklist is for you to spend a few minutes assessing your preparedness.

- ✔ Do you have someone with you who has wilderness first-aid or other first-aid competence?
- ✔ Does at least one member of the group have a skill level higher than the difficulty of the planned activity?
- ✔ Is everyone aware of what skills and fitness are required for the trip?
- ✔ Is everyone aware of what gear or safety equipment is practical and appropriate for the type of activity being done?
- ✔ Is training necessary for the activity?
- ✔ Will you need any specialized safety or rescue information?
- ✔ If you're using an instructor, outfitter, or resource person, have you checked her insurance, credentials, and references?
- ✔ Has at least one of the members of the group familiarized herself with the site or route?
- ✔ Has current information been obtained and reviewed, including seasonal differences in terrain or water levels?
- ✔ Do you have a compass and topographic maps and/or supplementary maps and route descriptions, and do one or more of you know how to read them and use a compass to find the way?
- ✔ Do you need to obtain permits—park, fire, and the like?

- ✔ Has everyone had the opportunity to educate herself thoroughly on all agreed upon plans, routes, and contingency plans prior to going?
- ✔ Prior to the trip, has the group discussed the expectations of each member as to her roles, if any, in the group?
- ✔ Are contingency funds available to the group?
- ✔ Has all equipment been checked to ensure that it's in safe, usable condition?
- ✔ Have you made instructions and safety information available to all group members, especially in regard to equipment that requires specific safety procedures—stoves, boats, rappelling equipment, and so on?
- ✔ Are you carrying repair supplies and backup items such as extra batteries, water purification tablets, magnesium strips, and so forth?
- ✔ Are safety support (emergency survival) kits available if the group is separated?
- ✔ Do you have deterrents for dangerous animals, and does the entire group know where they are and how to use them?
- ✔ Do you know the rudiments of backcountry weather prediction, especially the signs of impending storms?
- ✔ Is enough potable water available, or are you able to purify all aboveground water sources?
- ✔ If you're using a group kitchen and common food, does everyone with food allergies or dietary restrictions have safe meals?
- ✔ Can you place all food items and garbage in secure, animalproof containers away from the sleeping area and inaccessible to animals?
- ✔ Are you carrying a stocked first-aid kit that includes additional items for wilderness first-aid management, and does the entire group know where it's kept?
- ✔ Does the first-aid provider(s) know that she should make accurate records of any significant health care provided?
- ✔ Are the group members able to keep within a reasonably safe distance of each other in the backcountry?
- ✔ Does everyone know the methods of communication in the event of an emergency?
- ✔ Have you discussed the expectations of each group member as to her role in an emergency situation?

- ✔ Have you given the trip route and itinerary, including probable stopping points and expected return time, as well as the physical appearance of the group (members, tent colors, license plate numbers, and the like), to an emergency contact person?

- ✔ Have you let family/friends know who the emergency contact person is?

- ✔ Have you given the local authorities an itinerary and asked them to notify the group of any serious problems, such as weather conditions or forest fires expected in the area that the group will be traveling in?

- ✔ How will you notify the contact person holding the itinerary immediately upon your return?

Sample Kit List for Camping

Clothing

- ✔ Hat—a brim all around will provide better sun protection; lighter colors and lighter weights are most comfortable.
- ✔ Bandanna(s) (see page 25).
- ✔ Warm shirt to layer with—fleece or wool.
- ✔ T-shirts—long- and short-sleeved. Bring long-sleeved for sun protection if needed.
- ✔ Pants and shorts—not jeans. At least one pair should be made of quick-drying nylon or polyester.
- ✔ Sweat suit or fleece top and pants.
- ✔ Long underwear—not cotton.
- ✔ Underwear—if all you have is cotton, consider going without.
- ✔ Socks—bring extra socks, including one pair of wool or fleece.
- ✔ Lightweight jacket and a rain suit or a Gore-Tex jacket and pants—Gore-Tex will breathe.
- ✔ Bathing suit—if you'll be swimming.
- ✔ Appropriate footwear for the method of travel—hiking boots, riding boots, sneakers, or what have you.
- ✔ Lightweight sneakers, shoes, or sport sandals—to wear at the campsite and suitable for use in water if necessary. Sandals require an ankle strap.

Bedding

- ✔ Warm, lightweight bedroll waterproofed with a plastic garbage bag inside the stuff sack.
- ✔ Small foam sleeping pad or Therm-a-Rest.

Toiletries

- ✔ Small hairbrush or comb.
- ✔ Toothbrush (the airlines give away a great half-sized one in business class).
- ✔ Lip balm with sun protection.
- ✔ Other personal toiletry supplies as required.
- ✔ Small thin towel or chamois—not plush terry, which is heavy when wet and slow to dry.

Other

- ✔ Flashlight.
- ✔ 3 heavy-duty royal blue or orange garbage bags (see page 18).
- ✔ Whistle.
- ✔ Sunglasses with a string attachment.
- ✔ Personal water bottle—spillproof.
- ✔ Safety equipment needed for your type of activity or travel—helmets, gloves, personal flotation device (PFD), wetsuit, and the like.

Group Sharing

The group can share the following if you are shaving weight and no one has allergies or skin infections:

- ✔ Soap—biodegradable, vegetable-based, unscented.
- ✔ Unscented baby wipes.
- ✔ Toothpaste.
- ✔ Sunscreen—unscented.
- ✔ Bug repellent—nonaerosol (avoid too much DEET, which will eat away at your gear as well as your skin).

Optional Personal Gear

- ✔ Day pack—small and waterproof.

- ✔ Warm hat and gloves.
- ✔ Pocketknife.
- ✔ Compass.
- ✔ Camera.
- ✔ A small bag with clean clothes for traveling, toiletries, and makeup, left behind for use when you come out and clean up.

Group Equipment List

Items on this list are elaborated upon in other sections of this book, with tips on multiple uses, essential features, and weight considerations:

- ✔ Lightweight kitchen (see page 40).
- ✔ 2 lightweight stoves with a windscreen and/or a pot adapter, Esbit, or other pocket stove for backup.
- ✔ Fuel for stoves.
- ✔ Waterproofed matches, lighter, flint, magnesium strip, firestarters—three means of starting a fire are recommended.
- ✔ Cat-hole bag (see page 38).
- ✔ Water purifier and chemical purification tablets—have at least one method to purify water without boiling. Two is even better.
- ✔ Water carrier—coated nylon bags are the most lightweight, but there are lots of alternatives to choose from.
- ✔ Collapsible washbasin.
- ✔ Tents—as compact as possible. Sleeping should be cozy..
- ✔ Tarp and ropes (see pages 21–23 and 29–30).
- ✔ Rope with pulley—for caching (see page 57).
- ✔ Animal deterrent—pepper spray, popgun, flares or the like.
- ✔ First-aid kit (see pages 121–22).
- ✔ Safety support kits (see pages 48 and 120–21).
- ✔ Duct tape and any necessary equipment repair items (see page 19).
- ✔ Compass, map, and directions.

Optional Group Equipment

- ✔ A means of emergency communication that can be used where you will be traveling, if possible. Do not assume that your cell phone will work.

- ✓ Weather radio (see page 27)
- ✓ Large umbrella (see page 31)
- ✓ Large piece of heavy-duty foil, folded (see page 32)
- ✓ Firestarters (see page 32)

Safety Support Kit

I have always carried one of these kits, though I have never used one except to steal supplies occasionally. I don't like the scary "survival" mentality, so I've changed the name to the more proactive "Safety Support Kit" and continue to carry mine as a sort of security blanket.

The contents of the kit below are annotated as to their uses:

 – signaling

– health and safety

– warmth and shelter

– finding your way

In a waterproof container, hip sack, or stuff sack put:

- ✓ Bear bell on the outside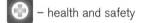
- ✓ Small air horn or loud whistle
- ✓ Flares (if traveling on water)
- ✓ Magnifying glass, unbreakable mirror, or CD-ROM
- ✓ 2 bright blue or orange garbage bags
- ✓ Emergency reflector blanket
- ✓ 4 feet of brightly colored trail tape
- ✓ Firestarters (cotton balls soaked in petroleum jelly and stuffed in a film container)
- ✓ Waterproof matches, lighter, magnesium strip (three ways of firestarting is recommended)
- ✓ Mini flashlight with extra bulb and batteries

- ✔ Candle (wrapped in plastic wrap) 🔺, ⚙
- ✔ Compass ⚙
- ✔ Copy of the map and directions ⚙
- ✔ 3 feet of duct tape wrapped around a waterproof marker 📶, ⚙, 🔺
- ✔ 10 feet of strong cord or dental floss ⚙, 🔺
- ✔ 1 or 2 energy bars ⚙
- ✔ Water purification tablets ⚙
- ✔ Condom (holds 1 quart of water) ⚙
- ✔ 2 clothespins ⚙, 🔺, 📶
- ✔ 4 large rubber bands to close cuffs 🔺
- ✔ Bandanna ⚙, 🔺
- ✔ Minor first-aid supplies in a snack-sized zipper-locking bag ⚙
    - Band-Aids
    - Antiseptic towelettes
    - Gauze pad
    - Needle and thread
    - Safety pins
    - Paper

Wilderness First-Aid Kit Group Supplies

Following is the list of contents for a first-aid kit. You can buy prepared kits, but you may want to add to them for backcountry use. Start with a 10-by-12-inch soft-sided kit and add to it where necessary:

- ✔ Scissors.
- ✔ Tweezers.
- ✔ Thermometer.
- ✔ 10 cc irrigation syringe.
- ✔ Safety pins.
- ✔ Needle and thread.
- ✔ Pocket mask or microshield.
- ✔ Latex gloves—several pairs.
- ✔ Small notebook and pencil.

- Maxi-pads—replaces the padding in a soft-sided bag.
- Topical antiseptic towelettes.
- Topical anesthetic cream.
- Topical antibiotic ointment.
- Aloe vera or other soothing gel.
- Baking soda in a small container.
- 1% hydrocortisone cream.
- Elastic fabric tensor bandage.
- Moleskin.
- Second Skin.
- 1-inch bandage strips.
- Finger cots.
- 2-by-2-inch and 4-by-4-inch sterile gauze pads.
- Nonadherent pads.
- Hypoallergenic cloth tape.
- Butterfly closures.
- SAM splints—if you can afford them.
- Cough drops.
- Tums (antacid).
- Pepto-Bismol.
- Imodium (antidiarrheal).
- Benadryl (antihistamine).
- Acetaminophen (analgesic).
- Ibuprofen (anti-inflammatory).
- Oralyte (rehydration salts).
- EpiPen (for life-threatening anaphylaxis or asthma attacks only—doctor's prescription required).
- Health information for all the participants in the group (contact and health insurance information, concerns, medications).
- Secondary survey checklist (see page 123)—I put a copy in the first-aid kit because I know I'll never remember it all if I need to.

Long-Term Remote First-Aid Survey Checklist

Casualty's Full Name _____

Primary
Airway OK? _____ Breathing OK? _____ Pulse Present? _____

Neck/Spine OK? _____ Excessive Bleeding Stopped? _____

What Happened?

What Signs Do You See?

What Does She Feel?

Head-to-toe Exam
Watch her face as you examine her. Note all tenderness, bruising, deformity, bleeding, swelling, loss of use, **anything unusual.**

Medic alert _____	Tightness _____
Head _____	Bloating _____
Eyes _____	Pelvis _____
Ears _____	Messed pants _____
Nose _____	Legs _____
Mouth _____	Joints normal _____
Face _____	Foot color _____
Face color _____	Foot temp (compare) _____
Breath odor _____	Feeling in feet _____
Sweating _____	Equal strength in feet _____
Neck _____	Arms/hands _____
Neck veins _____	Joints normal _____
Collarbones _____	Hand color _____
Ribs _____	Hand temp _____
Chest rise—both sides _____	Feeling in hands _____
Belly—4 quadrants _____	Equal grip _____

Notes on above:

Current medical conditions: Medications:

Significant past history: Allergies:

What do you think is wrong?

Treatment given: Describe exact treatment. Keep a complete record.

Vital Signs

Assess vital signs every 15 minutes in a stable casualty and every 3–5 minutes in an unstable casualty. Attach more sheets if necessary in order to document the casualty's condition until help arrives.

Time									
Pulse									
Breath rate									
Consciousness									
Pupils									
Skin									
Temperature									

Time									
Pulse									
Breath rate									
Consciousness									
Pupils									
Skin									
Temperature									

About the Author

Bobbi Hoadley lives and works in Vancouver, British Columbia, with her husband and two daughters. She is the camping writer/editor for the national magazine of the Girl Guides of Canada/Guides du Canada and has helped develop new girl camping programs, outdoor leader training programs, and a risk management framework for the organization. She transcends her busy life as often as possible with canoeing, kayaking, and camping of any sort.